Dynamic Technical Analysis

Dynamic Technical Analysis

Philippe Cahen

JOHN WILEY & SONS, LTD
Chichester · New York · Weinheim · Brisbane · Singapore · Toronto

Other Wiley Editorial Offices

John Wiley & Sons, Inc., 605 Third Avenue,
New York, NY 10158-0012, USA

Wiley-VCH Verlag GmbH, Pappelallee 3,
D-69469 Weinheim, Germany

John Wiley & Sons (Australia) Ltd, 33 Park Road, Milton,
Queensland 4064, Australia

John Wiley & Sons (Asia) Pte Ltd, 2 Clementi Loop #02-01,
Jin Xing Distripark, Singapore 129809

John Wiley & Sons (Canada) Ltd, 22 Worcester Road,
Rexdale, Ontario M9W 1L1, Canada

Library of Congress Cataloging-in-Publication Data
Cahen, Philippe.
     [Analyse technique dynamique. English]
     Dynamic technical analysis / Philippe Cahen.
         p. cm.—(The Wiley trading advantage series)
     Includes bibliographical references and index.
     ISBN 0-471-89947-X (cloth)
         1. Stock price forecasting—Mathematical models. 2. Investment analysis—Mathematical
models. I. Title. II. Wiley trading advantage.
     HG4637.C34 2000
     332.63'222'0112—dc21   00-025347

British Library Cataloguing in Publication Data
A catalogue record for this book is available from the British Library

ISBN 0-471-89947-X

Typeset in 12/14pt Palatino by C.K.M. Typesetting, Salisbury, Wiltshire
Printed and bound in Great Britain by Biddles Ltd, Guildford and King's Lynn
This book is printed on acid-free paper responsibly manufactured from sustainable forestry, in which
at least two trees are planted for each one used for paper production.

Contents

Foreword

In a world where relatively little has been written about Bollinger bands, Philippe Cahen's book comes as a pleasant surprise. I first met Mr Cahen at the 1995 annual seminar of the International Federation of Technical Analysts in San Francisco, where he presented me with a copy of his first book on Bollinger bands, *Gagner avec l'Analyse Technique Dynamique*. Although the book was in French, which I spoke as a child but alas do not speak now, I was able to understand the basic principles he espoused through a careful perusal of the illustrations and the bit of the text I could puzzle out.

One of the great joys of having invented an analytical technique such as Bollinger bands is seeing what other people do with it. Mr Cahen sits on a Credit Lyonnais trading desk where, in the course of the firm's dealing activities, he is required to give instant and accurate appraisals of a large number of diverse financial instruments. To do this he has developed a framework using daily, weekly and monthly Bollinger band charts accompanied by indicators such as Gerald Appel's moving average convergence–divergence (MACD) and George Lane's stochastics. With these techniques, he is able to render a rigorous opinion in short order, along with price targets and critical levels to watch.

Mr Cahen's newest work, translated here into English for the first time, extends his prior work and explains the techniques he uses in his day-to-day analysis. A broad range of techniques and strategies are covered, supported by charts that clarify the text.

Concepts such as bubbles and parallels will be familiar to anybody who has looked at Bollinger bands with any degree of curiosity. However, some of their implications regarding trends may be eye-openers for many. Few have understood the forecasting implications of changing volatility, though Bollinger bands make this aspect of the evolution of the price structure clearly evident. By drawing a distinction between sustainable and unsustainable moves, Mr Cahen draws attention to this important aspect of the price structure.

Another interesting aspect of Mr Cahen's work is the comparison of price action within the bands and indicator action. This is the area in which I have done most of my work and it is a great pleasure to see another analyst demonstrate the power of this approach. Especially interesting is his use of the band structure to determine which indicators to base decisions on. One area completely new to me is the addition of Welles Wilder's stop mechanism, parabolics – sometimes known as stop and reverse – and the study of their relationship to Bollinger bands.

Mr Cahen's emphasis on multiple time frames is an extremely important facet of his work. He uses the classical technical analysis framework, days, weeks and months, allowing one period to inform another in his triptych. I have long advocated the use of short-, intermediate- and long-term time frames, and it is gratifying to see those ideas deployed successfully here.

Recently I had the pleasure of speaking with Mr Cahen in Paris at a one-day seminar sponsored by Waldata. I had a chance to learn of the latest developments and twists in his work. I found them very interesting and in at least one case quite challenging. In short, hearing Mr Cahen's talk made me think – what more could I ask? I hope that reading this book will make you think – after all, what more could you ask?

John Bollinger, CFA, CMT   2 December 1999
Bollinger Capital Management, Inc
www.BollingerBands-com

Preface

The present edition is an update of the French second edition. It takes account of a number of comments made by contributors to Internet user groups as well as of some recent improvements to the *Dynamic Technical Analysis of Financial Markets* (DTAFM®) method itself. One of these offers a means of forecasting trend reversals, which shows an impressive success rate when large-scale swings are taking place in prices or indices. This means that the method now gives even more accurate forecasts, whether for intraday trades or when trading out to several days or weeks ahead.

Acknowledgements

By encouraging analysts to integrate volatility – a variable that has become critical – into forecasting models, John Bollinger deserves the grateful thanks of technical analysts the world over. Bollinger bands and their applications have helped technical analysis to evolve, to become a permanent fixture of the financial landscape, and to achieve credibility as we move into the new millennium.

Purists will, of course, point to erroneous usage from a statistical standpoint, and can easily back up their claims. Let us, however, be pragmatic, and look once again at the merits of the model and the approach. Traders who use Bollinger bands regularly make significant capital gains. This was the target John Bollinger set himself, and he has achieved his goal. Yet his model goes further, because when sharp swings in stock prices are observed, Bollinger bands are the simplest and most effective means for investors to retain control over the situation. What is more, John Bollinger's research has enabled technical analysts to build the concept of market volatility into their models. Such volatility has come to play a far greater role in recent years due to technological advances. These changes are not related to the business cycle, but are genuinely structural changes. John has opened up a whole new avenue and continues to explore it. For my part, I have chosen to follow a path parallel to his, using his materials. Without detracting from his achievement, I am joining forces with him in hoping that others will also use his research and ensure that it remains familiar to all investors who use technical analysis models for many years to come.

I would also like to thank Jean-Paul Betbéze, Head of Economic and Financial Research at Crédit Lyonnais, for his invaluable advice. Special thanks also to Esther M. Baroudy, Senior Analyst, International Fixed Income Portfolios, GE Investments (US) Ltd, for her penetrating comments and critical reading of the text.

All the graphs prepared for this book were computer-generated using Walmaster Gold software (Waldata, Immeuble le Vivaldi, 87 route de Grigny, 91130 Ris-Orangis, France; tel. +33 1 69 02 75 00, www.walmaster.com). Finally, I would like to thank Eric Walker and his team for lavishing all the necessary care and attention needed to ensure the correct graphical interpretation of my DTAFM® method.

Chapter 1

Introduction

The DTAFM$^{®}$ method is aimed at two types of trader: the speculator[1] and the long-term investor.[2] It will help investors to judge the best moment to take up or unwind a market position, and to compare the fluctuation potential of several securities or markets thanks to a single unit of measure used across the complete spectrum of financial products – futures contracts, stock indices, domestic or international securities, currencies, commodities, and so on. In some cases, investors will put on their speculators' hats when price fluctuations widen considerably, enabling them to optimize management of their profits. Speculators, on the other hand, will find a structured system they can use to take up positions only when strong price fluctuations are expected, in time frames of anything from ten minutes to several weeks.

1.1. Benefits of Dynamic Analysis

If you want to employ a particular method to earn money, that method has to allow you to make forecasts and not just observations of existing patterns. Until the early 1980s, market fluctuations were limited in scope. The trading methods used did not need to take the impact of potential sharp volatility-driven market swings[3] into account when making forecasts. At present (and for the foreseeable future), it is will be essential to take large-scale volatility into account as well as drastic changes in its nature and direction, together with the possibility that markets can become seriously agitated after a period of calm, and vice versa.

Observing patterns from a static viewpoint offers only a partial vision of the market. This is one of the causes of the impasse in which mainstream technical analysis finds itself, and is partly due to the very limited technical resources at the disposal of analysts and the fact that their methods have changed little since 1932. With advances in information technology since 1990, researchers have been able to develop new concepts. Thus, by taking the behaviour of various categories of trader simultaneously into account, the indicators can be analysed from a dynamic angle, exploring changes in the state of the indicators themselves, and changes to them along a time line. We intend to leverage these concepts to make forecasts and imbue them with a reliability and lifespan that no traditional method can equal. After all, why use the value of these indicators at a given point in time to underpin our forecasts? It could be justified in terms of improving communication if their value remained constant. But what interests operators is to find out where the markets are heading when prices start trending. In this case, the values assigned by the analyst only hold true at the time when the analysis is made. At $t + x$, the computed objectives are wrong.

In Figure 1.1, on the left-hand curve, prices are stable. If the indicator represented by line 1 shows a crossover, prices can be expected to fall. Between points 2 and 3, the value of the indicator was stable. The target (i.e., the value of the indicator) fixed at point 2 is unchanged at point 3, so use of the indicator value at point 2 does not result in an error of strategy. However, on the right-hand curve, we note a sharp uptrend. If indicator 4 is not used as a support level, the drop will accelerate. Traders thus take up a buy position at point 5 and unwind it if the price crosses through the indicator. At point 6, the value at which the trader must abandon his position is no longer the support breakthrough value calculated at point 5. If the trader

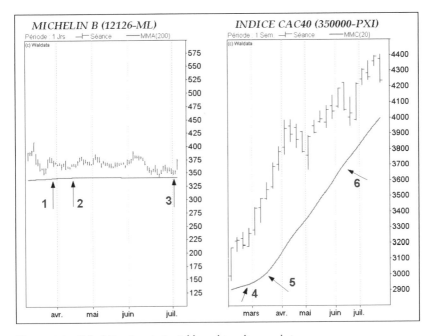

Figure 1.1   Calculating targets in stable and trending markets.

expects to find the same value at 6 as he found at 5, he will make a substantial loss. The use of the numerical value leads the trader into a very serious trading error because he has not used his model to unwind the position, otherwise he would have applied the indicator value at point 6 and turned a profit. Retaining the value computed at point 5 as a forecast is no different from picking a number at random. The target set at point 5 is useless. All the trader has is an observation of what has happened at points 2 and 5. So when there is a marked market trend, the stronger the trend, the more mistaken the numerical forecasts.

To get round this problem, we recommend setting the indicators themselves as objectives. Forecasts will thus be automatically updated as prices change. The indicators are designated by upper-case letters, while the unit of time[4] of the particular graph will be added to it to avoid making reading errors.

This notation system allows us to make an easy comparison between different products, since buy and sell signals will be triggered on crossing a target indicator, and not from a given value in a nominal unit of measure. In a specific sector, the various values will all intersect a given indicator at the same time. Elf, for example, will cross a particular threshold at the same time as Total and the per-barrel oil price. This principle is also used to strengthen risk management.

1.2. States of a Market

When we observe the historical series of prices representing market fluctuations, we see two possible states: stable or trending. The trend is either an uptrend or a downtrend. To decide which it is, all one has to do is look at the direction of a moving average[5] over 20 periods. This is always represented on the price chart. In the left-hand section of Figure 1.2, the moving average is flat at point 1. There is no trend. In the centre, the moving average at point 2 is moving upwards, revealing an uptrend; while on the right, the moving average at point 3 is on a downtrend.

When the market is stable, traders will rely more on an indicator. When there is a marked market trend (up or down) they will be guided by other indicators. It is also worth making a distinction between a modest and a strong trend, because although such trends have been regularly observed for many years past on specific markets such as the currency and commodity markets, they have been impacting all markets for the past few years, including those for so-called "gilt-edged" stocks. Any trader, whether a professional or an individual investor, will thus sooner or later be confronted with a market showing a strong or very strong trend.

As soon as operators are aware of the criteria for qualifying a market trend (stable, weak or strong), their forecasts, using simple, specific models, because they are targeted, become effective rather than random.

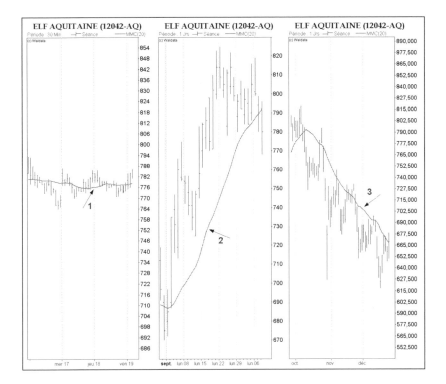

Figure 1.2   Stable, rising and falling markets.

The simpler the method, the easier it is to understand and implement.

1.3. Needs of the Different Types of Trader

All too often, analysts generate the graph of a given product using a daily bar chart, and then use it willy-nilly as the basis either for a two-month forward analysis or for the next day. This leads people to believe that there is no other way to present the product concerned and that a daily chart can be used to make forecasts for any old time horizon. Things work differently in the real world. If you look at the charts used by the different classes of player, you will see that professional speculators track market movements using sub-hourly charts, whereas others use charts whose major unit of time[6] is one month. Six different major units of time can be identified, and these are shown in Table 1.1.

To generate profits, it is important to get your forecasting horizon right, so you must have a good idea of the major unit of time that best suits your objectives.

Since there are six different units of time, this means that there is not just one dollar/euro exchange rate, or one CAC 40 index, but six dollar/euro exchange rates and six CAC 40 indices, whose objectives are independent of each other. Thus, there is no reason why the Elf share shown using a daily unit of time should at any given time present the same trend as the same share shown on a monthly time scale.

Figure 1.3 shows the Elf share at end-1997, using a monthly time scale on the left and a daily one on the right. In the left-hand chart,

Table 1.1   Units of time* for tracking market movements.

Transaction duration Forecast time horizon	Unit of time	Type of market	Category of player
	5 minutes		Control unit
15 minutes to 2 hours	10 minutes	Forex	Professional speculators
2 to 5 hours	30 minutes	Futures markets (fixed income, forex)	Dealing room traders
4 to 6 hours	60 minutes	Futures markets (equities, indices)	Dealing room traders, individual speculators
2 to 7 days	1 day	All markets	
1 to 3 weeks	1 week	All markets	
3 weeks to 2 months	1 month	All markets	
3 to 8 months	1 quarter	All markets	

*In the DTAFM® system, the following abbreviations are used:
Q for quarterly   30 for thirty minutes
M for monthly   10 for ten minutes
W for weekly   5 for five minutes
D for daily
H for hourly

Figure 1.3   Monthly and daily time scale.

the moving average reveals an uptrend, whereas in the right-hand chart, it is on a downtrend.

The concepts of investor and speculator do not simply refer to the time frame envisaged for a transaction. Investors generally do not take positions for less than a week and therefore use a major unit of time of a day or more. Speculators can also take up a position using a weekly major unit of time. In some cases, moreover, market conditions will allow an investor to take a position and generate substantial capital gains even when the specific criteria for speculative trades do not exist. In this case, speculators will not be able to take up a position. Generally speaking, the idea is not to take advantage of all price moves in order to make a profit, but to enable traders either to make money when the opportunity arises, or else to optimize the time at which they enter a market. This method helps you make substantial gains with minimum risk, when market trends correspond exactly to the configurations described in the following pages. Once the trader feels confident with the models, he or she will be able to trade and become independent of the environment. Apart from the good results obtained, a significant decrease in the amount of time devoted to analysis can be put to good use either to seek out other opportunities or to do other things.

1.4. Trend Correction or Reversal

This is another point to remember. When a market reverses, it is important to realize the nature of the upcoming trend. There are two possibilities: a correction or technical recovery; or a full-blown trend reversal. Figure 1.4 shows a change of trend taking place at point 1; at point 2 what we have is merely a correction.

When confronted with a trend reversal, it is essential to unwind the previous position and at the same time to reverse it. In the case of a technical correction/recovery, you should leave the position unchanged if the major unit of time is hourly or sub-hourly. Price fluctuations in this case are not sufficient to cover brokerage fees. On longer units of time, the response should be the same in principle, although experience shows that traders generally like to play the trend. They should, however, realize that they are taking a certain risk.

On the left in Figure 1.5 (monthly time scale), the index fell from 3100 at point 1 to 2450 at point 2. On the right (30-minute time scale) the price fell from 734 at point 3 to 726 at point 4. If brokerage fees are sufficiently low to allow you to make a turn on trades carried out between points 1 and 2, the same cannot be said for the other deal.

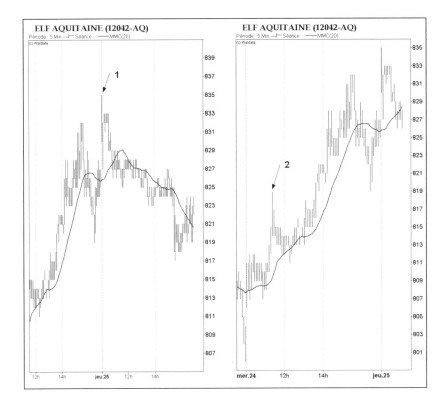

Figure 1.4   Trend reversal and technical correction/recovery.

1.5. Conclusion

I have touched on all the main factors contributing to decision-making. They are few but essential. Taking the different categories of traders and their interaction into account offers a complete market picture at any given moment. I shall be referring to these throughout the following pages. In the chapters to come, I will explain how to distinguish between corrections and trend reversals.

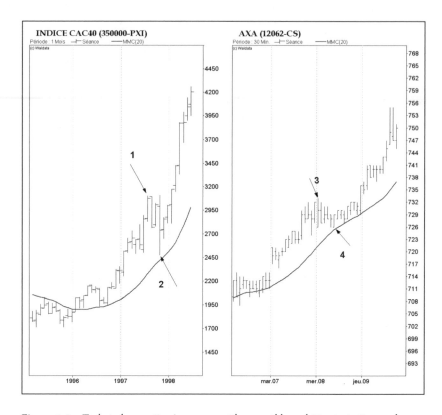

Figure 1.5   Technical correction/recovery, with a monthly and 30-minute time scale.

Notes

1. A person who seeks to take advantage of stock-price spreads due to market volatility, regardless of the transaction time frame – which can be anything from a few minutes to a few years.
2. A person seeking to enter a market with different aims from the speculator (investment, risk hedging, trading, etc.).
3. This applies not only to stock market indices, but also to securities, futures contracts, currencies and commodities alike.
4. The unit of time is used as a reference for the forecast time frame. This will depend on the length of time during which price fluctuations are recorded on a bar chart to form a graph. Bar charts show a vertical line representing the highest and lowest prices quoted during a certain time period, with starting prices on the left and closing prices on the right. The period corresponds to the number of bar charts taken into

account. For example, a unit of time can be an hour, a week or whatever, just as a bar chart can be hourly, weekly or whatever. A period of 9 will comprise the last nine bar charts. In the example, therefore, this means nine consecutive hours of trading or nine weeks.

5. A statistical tool that smooths price fluctuations. A moving average gives some idea as to whether a trend is moving up, down or flatlining. Moreover, by combining a moving average with an indicator, it is possible to pick up trend direction changes.

6. In the DTAFM$^{\text{\textregistered}}$ method, the major unit of time corresponds to the forecast horizon. The principal unit of time is the next unit of time up from the major unit of time. The control unit of time is the next unit of time down from the major unit of time.

Chapter 2

Methodology

The DTAFM® method takes the interaction of different categories of trader into account. This was not possible before 1992 because of the limited storage capacity of computers. Because the method was developed for trading purposes, the results are excellent using longer forecasting horizons. A widespread phenomenon in technical analysis is that a method always delivers better results using longer time periods that those it was designed for. Methods developed before 1970, at a time when intraday transactions were marginal, have consequently become completely obsolete. My approach is based above all on prudential principles, taking into account the specific nature of each type of trader, the transaction time frame and the state of the market in which the trader is operating.

2.1. Safety

DTAFM® seeks to make available a series of consistent models allowing you to make profits when the market trends upward, downwards or even, in some circumstances, when it is stable. To achieve this, several indicators are used simultaneously. Since the market can be in one of two states (stable or trending) you should use the indicators most suited to each state.

Figure 2.1 shows two complementary indicators. Below the price line on the left-hand graph (stable market), the crossovers of the central indicator and its average, used to trigger buy and sell signals, are clearer and give better results than the lower indicator. On the right-hand graph (trending market), the reverse is true. This shows that you cannot use a single indicator to manage different market states. However, the approach is identical whether the graph shows a stock, a currency, an interest rate future or a commodity.

The information provided by the most volatile indicator should be used to analyse the market when it is stable. Because the fluctuations will only be small-scale, you will need to use an indicator that acts as a magnifier in order to apprehend the microscopic price changes.

The other indicator will be used in a trending market.

When a market reversal signal is given by the more volatile indicator and confirmed by a signal from the other indicator, traders

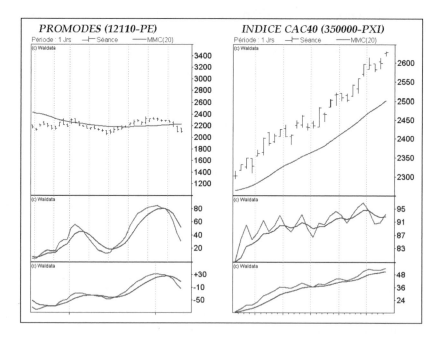

Figure 2.1   Prices and indicators.

may take action knowing that this cannot be because of a mistaken interpretation. At a later stage, if the market is virtually flat, we use the volatile indicator to track the market. If a strong trend develops, the first indicator will very quickly be saturated and become useless. At that point, the other indicator allows you to track the market. Similarly, if you want to unwind the position, depending on the way the market is moving, other specific indicators will be used.

2.2. Trading in the Markets

It would be misleading to claim that you cannot make mistakes using DTAFM®. We do know, however, under which conditions these are likely to occur and we can alert you to them, allowing you to respond quickly to minimize any losses. Remember that you do not judge the validity of a method from a single trade but from a whole series. To be useful, a method has to deliver positive results — minimum losses and maximum profits. On the other hand, you should avoid using a method that does not stop you from making large-scale losses, even if this only happens occasionally.

Markets are increasingly volatile. During the first quarter of 1998, stocks on the French Monthly Settlement market exhibited wider fluctuations than the currency markets did only three years earlier. Moreover, at certain periods, the trends offer large-scale visibility in terms of fluctuation variation, while the opposite can be observed at other times. A 1997 press article about the CAC 40 index of French blue chips[1] forecast that a sharp drop would be followed by a sharp rise in 1998. But by April 1998, long-term visibility on the CAC 40 was limited to fluctuations of 4–5%.

I am often asked how reliable the method is. The answer is that it all depends on how you apply it. I know that this isn't really an answer, so I will try and explain, especially as successful use of the DTAFM® method is largely contingent on this. There are two possible situations, depending on whether the user is an investor or a speculator. DTAFM® is used by investors to determine the best time to take up or unwind a position. In such situations, users have a time frame and, in general, a restricted range of products. The result will consequently depend partly on decisions they cannot influence. The time constraints involved in taking up a position mean they have to use the signals of two complementary indicators when taking a position. These are the stochastic and the moving average convergence–divergence (MACD).

The issues are different in the case of speculators, since they are completely independent. Although they may not necessarily be free to choose their products or securities, they do have complete freedom when it comes to taking a position when they want. And although management rules are obviously necessary in this case, the fact remains that they enjoy considerable latitude. Before making a trade, they will wait until they see particular configurations signalling a strong trend. Here, two other indicators are more appropriate: the parabolic and Bollinger bands. On intraday trading, we have observed very high success levels, and on monthly time frames a success rate of 80% has been observed. Losses are generally limited to 3% of capital. Gains, on the other hand, can be extremely substantial and since the whole idea of using DTAFM® is to make money, we actively seek out specific configurations. Using some of these, a strong price movement can be forecast in almost 90% of cases. Losses in this case are generally due to users not complying with decision-making criteria. Sometimes, the loss is due to the stop-loss order systematically placed whenever a position is taken. The software, too, can be a source of errors and in due course I will suggest ways of dealing with this problem. Other configurations will help you anticipate continued price stagnation. That does not stop you from setting objectives at any time on any market, but I think it is preferable to make an effort when it is worthwhile. Once again, remember that the one who should get rich is the trader, and not the financial intermediary who pockets the brokerage fees!

2.3. Triptych

It is absolutely essential to use the triptych if you want to get the best out of DTAFM®. Earlier, I said that a single stock or index could show a certain trend on a given unit of time and another trend, even an opposing trend, on a different unit of time. This means that operators must always be aware of their environment. Keeping an eye on configurations using neighbouring units of time will provide information that could be vitally important. Analysis of the principal unit of time provides information about the underlying trend of the major unit of time you are using. The control unit of time optimizes the most opportune time to trade. An investor seeking to take a position must therefore take three graphs into account, not one. Moreover, the control unit of time also plays an important safety-net role when an operator makes a speculative trade.

Representation

On the left in Figure 2.2, prices are given using a monthly unit of time, which here serves as the principal unit of time. The stochastic is always depicted below the priceline, and the MACD at the bottom. The central graph is weekly. This is the major unit of time, and the forecasting horizon is thus between one and three weeks. On the right is the control unit of time (day). Although this involves three times more work than usual, it doesn't take three times longer to carry out the analyses because they are similar. As a rule of thumb, we have noticed that a person who has around 30 hours' experience with DTAFM® can analyse and reproduce results for 40 stocks, indices or currencies on a spreadsheet within 40 minutes or so.

Rules to Follow

The major unit of time must suit your own particular needs. In other

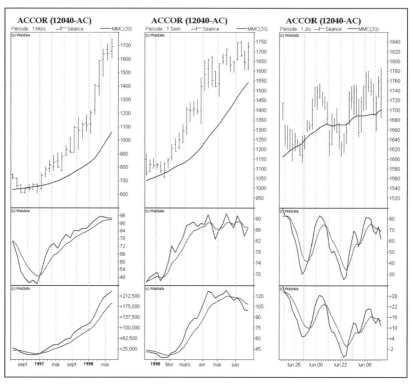

Figure 2.2 Triptych.

words, if you prefer the control unit of time when analysing the triptych you should ask yourself a number of questions. As a general rule, people do this when the major unit of time is weekly. Traders without access to real-time data are tempted to base their decisions on weekly graphs. Using a control unit of time as the major unit of time can only lead to failure. The solution might be to switch to software offering real-time prices, if the cost of the database is compatible with the size of the portfolio under management. If the investment is too expensive, you have to accept that you can only get daily updates and make only a few trades each year on a specific market. But by trawling through your database, you will regularly find opportunities, because of the almost daily appearance of new products that are starting to take off. However, what most individual investors expect from technical analysis is to be able to make one trade per week. In this case, the triptych must comprise a weekly principal unit of time, a daily major unit of time, and an hourly unit of control. This limitation has nothing to do with the method. The emergence of deferred real time means a new category of speculator can enter the field: individual speculators. These are people who want to generate capital gains over periods of a few days, while only checking out their software once a day (this is the basic need of most individuals who use technical analysis). They will use a weekly, daily and hourly triptych. They will have opportunities of finding many signals related to the speculation/stock-picking option without increasing the cost of using their software and staying glued to their screens. The lion's share of short-term trades are carried out by professionals who use hourly or sub-hourly graphs. These fluctuations are observed in real time.

By observing the following rules, investors will ensure that taking up a position does not result in significant losses.

Never trade against the trend shown by the principal unit of time.

To take up a position, wait until the trend is identical on the major unit of time and the control unit of time.

The rules can be adjusted depending on the length of the major unit of time, but this increases the risk of error. Using a weekly major unit of time, price fluctuations might be sufficiently wide to offer a degree of flexibility in the application of the rule about the comparison with the principal unit of time. Similarly, if the control unit is daily, you can take a position if the overbought/oversold state of the unit of time came about during the days preceding the crossover on the major unit of time. In this case, you must make sure that the central indicator is running parallel to its moving average and that this situation will continue over the next few days. The longer the time between the crossover of the indicator located in the bottom of the major unit of time and the one in the bottom of the control unit of time, the greater the risk. But since this notion is relative, you can make a decision based on an analysis of the time series of the market involved. With a weekly major unit of time, these conditions exist no more than once or twice a year on a given market. However, you can expect an average gain of 15% for each trade. If the number of in/out trades does not necessarily correspond to the number of trades it is possible to make using technical analysis, the potential results can nevertheless match everybody's hopes. By using a shorter unit of time, you increase the potential for making speculative trades, trading more often, and consequently expecting higher gains.

Speculators should use the control unit of time as a "stop-loss" in order to limit losses when the market does not respond as expected.

Look for the Outstanding Nugget of Information in the Triptych

I mention this so soon because every explanation in the rest of the book can help you identify that crucial piece of information. Some items of information will be second-rate, while others will be genuine "scoops" for the analyst, and will be used to support your analysis. To draw a comparison, imagine that you are standing in a room containing 200 paintings. It won't take you more than a quarter of a minute to see one that stands out from all the others, either because it is so ugly or in such bad taste or, more likely, because of its beauty, harmony or mystery. The same spirit should govern your analysis of the triptych. Either you immediately come across a capital item of information, and you will be able to develop your forecast thanks to this numerical clue, or else you will not come across any outstanding item of data, in which case there is no point in wasting any further time on that particular triptych. If you find several major items of data on the same graph, you should always give more weight to the one in the longest unit of time. Subsequently, when you come to draw up your forecast, you will need to construct its "once and future history", and to do this, you will need to imagine how the indicators are going to evolve. Here again, you must remember that these mental gymnastics are designed to help you make money. You will only select those scenarios in which large-scale price fluctuations are likely. This means you will select securities that have a glowing future. At the end of this book, we will construct one of these histories. But it seems you will take to the discipline more readily if, before you start out, you know what you will be asked to do at some later stage.

The approach used in making forecasts is similar to that of a game of strategy. You need to imagine how the main factors are likely to evolve and which are the possibly preponderant factors, and what that implies.

2.4. Different Approaches by Investors and Speculators

The indicators used by each category of trader are the same, but they apply them differently. The criteria used to decide whether to enter a market or not are specific to each type of player. That said, all traders have the same objective once they have taken a position – to make the maximum gain. So investors and speculators will use the same approach and the same tools to manage and unwind a position.

Note

1. *Agefi*, 25 August 1997.

Chapter 3

Indicators Used with DTAFM®

Two types of indicator are used — cyclical indicators and a number of models derived from moving averages. The former are the main tools used by investors, and serve as safety-net tools by speculators. The second group of models is used by all market participants to define support and resistance levels. These are used by speculators to take out positions. They also help to manage a position and unwind it when large-scale price swings are expected.

3.1. Cyclical Indicators

Shared Characteristics

Two indicators are used, members of the same family. Although their algorithms are different, and they both have their unique characteristics, they are represented and interpreted in the same way.

Objectivity

One of the strengths of these models is their ease of use. Buy/sell signals can only become effective when an indicator has crossed its moving average. Thus, all observers can identify a buy or sell signal at the same point in time. A certain number of criteria specific to the shape of the crossover enable participants to qualify the nature of the expected move.

Crossovers

Not all crossovers between an indicator and its moving average take place in the same way, just as a crossover that might have taken place but did not tells the analyst things about the current trend. Two parameters are taken into account: the angle formed at the time of the indicator's reversal and the type of crossover. When a crossover involving an indicator and its moving average is not clear-cut, you should not try to draw any conclusions.

Angle

The angle formed when the indicator changes direction is the most significant factor. The more acute the angle, the bigger the move is likely to be. However, more often than not, the indicator's trend change takes place only gradually and the acute angle is generally rounded.

Types of crossover

Two factors are important: how fast the moving average draws parallel with the indicator, and the time lag between the sharp end of the indicator's reversal and the point where the crossover between the indicator and its moving average takes place. Crossovers between an indicator and its moving average break down into four types.

Type I: new strong trend (Figure 3.1). The indicator reversal is severe and a sharp angle is often observed. The moving average crosses over the indicator very rapidly near the apex and the two curves quickly draw parallel.

Type II: new weak trend (Figure 3.2). The indicator reversal takes place gradually. Before starting a new trend, the indicator curve flatlines for a short period. Although the crossover with the moving average does not occur a long way from the point, it has nevertheless been observed that the moving average takes some time to move parallel with the indicator.

Type III: strong technical recovery/correction (Figure 3.3). The flat-line lasts a little longer. The main difference is due to the fact that the indicator immediately tries to cross back over the moving average in the opposite direction. The moving average has a difficult time reverting to the direction of the indicator.

Type IV: weak technical recovery/correction (Figure 3.4). In addition to a crossover between the indicator and its moving average, some distance from the apex, this type of crossover features repeated attempts by the indicator to cross back over its moving average once more. The moving average cannot change trend.

Crossovers are not identical for all products and on all units of time. They can be calibrated by analysing the historic series of each market.

Management[1]

This word is used to quantify[2] the weighting of the investment used for buy/sell trades. When several criteria are used simultaneously, the one with the highest weighting will be chosen. Information of this type is used by analysts to support or fine-tune their conclusions. Some criteria can also be used in conjunction with weightings depending on market configuration.

The type of crossover is a criterion equal to 50. If the crossover is of type I, the weighting is 100% of the criterion; if type II, 70%; if type III, 30%; and if type IV, 0%.

False crossover

In their haste to make recommendations, analysts are sometimes led into errors of interpretation, and this is the main cause of mistakes

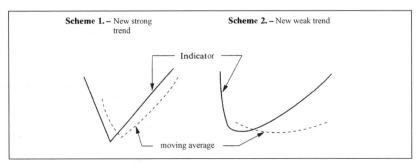

Figure 3.1   New strong trend.   **Figure 3.2**   New weak trend.

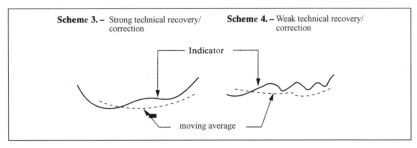

Figure 3.3   Strong technical recovery/   **Figure 3.4**   Weak technical recovery/
correction.   correction.

committed with the method. The error can arise on both indicators. To be valid, a crossover has to be observed after the first price quote in a new period. During the period, a crossover may appear and disappear as prices move, but it should not be taken into account before the start of the next period. The problem is less acute for a trader working with a ten-minute major unit of time than for some-one using a weekly major unit of time. The former will only have to wait for a few minutes before the next period begins, while the latter may perhaps have to wait five days. If the crossover disappears before the end of the period, what you have seen is a non-crossover. The market trend will at that point be the opposite of the one for which the position was taken.

In the central chart of Figure 3.5 the stochastic has stopped falling, but it is still a long way from the moving average several minutes after the start of trading.

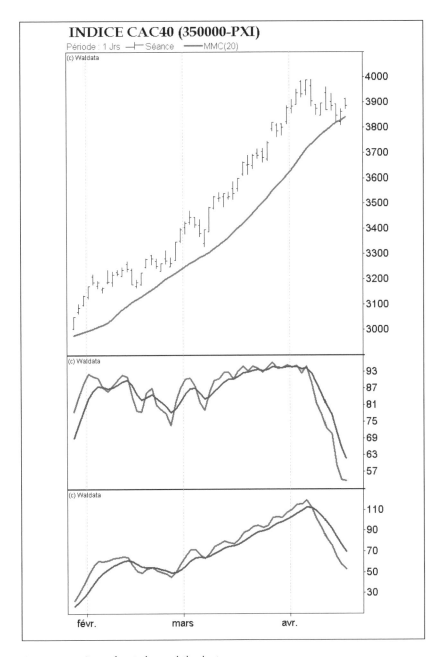

Figure 3.5   Start of period on a daily chart.

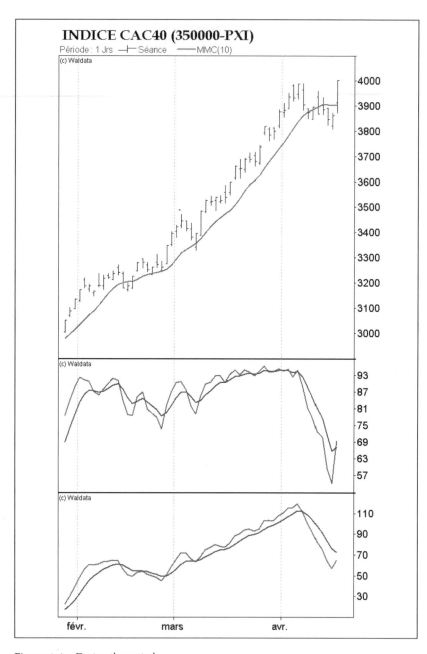

Figure 3.6   During the period.

In Figure 3.6, prices have risen quite sharply during the day. The previous top has even been exceeded. The stochastic has crossed its moving average. For the signal to be valid, however, the trader has to wait for the end of the period because, until the end of the day, further fluctuations might invalidate the crossover. Conversely, if the crossover is still visible after the start of the next period (the following day in this case), the probability that the signal will disappear rapidly decreases.

The left-hand part of Figure 3.7 shows the market situation at the close. Prices have fallen back to a level close to that at the start of trading. The crossover has disappeared and the trend is still bearish. The right-hand part of Figure 3.7 shows the situation a few days later. The aborted crossover on the stochastic has transformed into a non-crossover and the downtrend has accelerated.

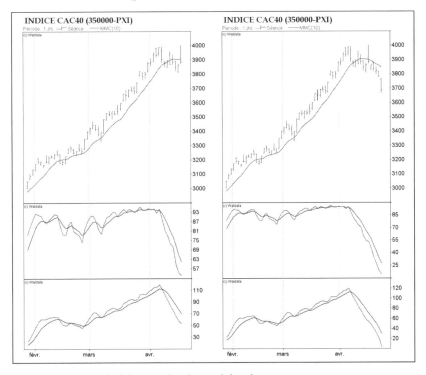

Figure 3.7   The end of the period and several days later.

Non-crossover

This is a failed attempt at a crossover between the indicator and its moving average. Generally, a crossover is observed after the start of a time period, but has disappeared at the end of the period. This happens when an item of important news is not in line with trader expectations, or when a persistent rumour is denied, for example. A non-crossover can also be observed over a unit of time if on the lower unit of time the crossover is type III or IV.

The effect of a non-crossover between an indicator and its moving average is to strengthen the earlier trend. If the main trend is up, a non-crossover can be assimilated to an overbought state immediately succeeded by an oversold state. If the main trend is down, a non-crossover points to an oversold state immediately succeeded by an overbought state. I mentioned earlier that the phenomena observed on the stochastic are linked to small-scale movements, whereas those observed on the MACD signal strong moves. The presence of a non-crossover on the stochastic triggers a less powerful strengthening of the main trend than if it is observed on the MACD. Where a non-crossover is observed simultaneously on both models, this indicates a strengthening of the previous trend. Non-crossovers play an important role in this method, and I shall provide further information about non-crossover effects when I come to analyse other indicators.

In Figure 3.8, once non-crossover A has ended, a sharp rise follows the correction at 1—2.

Crossover confirmation

The stochastic indicator is used to observe fluctuations on a stable market because it is highly volatile. The crossover between the stochastic and its moving average occurs before the crossover seen on the MACD. You must not take a position before a crossover observed on the stochastic has been confirmed by a crossover on the MACD. Safety has a price, after all. In such conditions you will never be able to buy at the low and sell at the peak, but at least you will avoid acting on a lot of false signals.

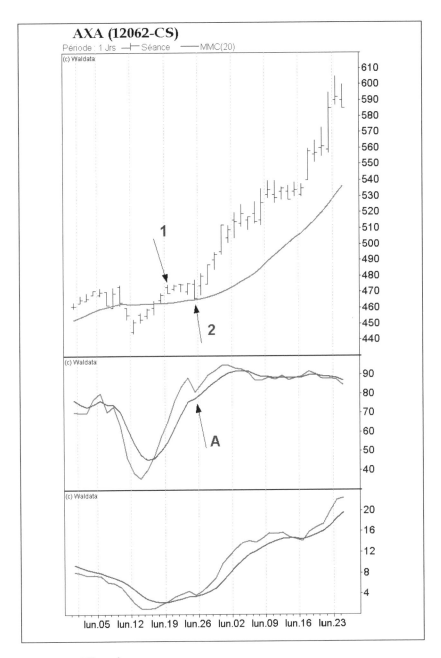

Figure 3.8 Effect of a non-crossover.

Overbought/oversold

This indicates a changing trend. It can signal either a technical move or a trend reversal.

Definition

When an indicator (stochastic or MACD) crosses its moving average, the market is overbought if the moving average moves above the indicator. If it is the indicator which moves above its moving average, the market is said to be oversold.

Not all overbought or oversold states are interesting to analyse, because they mainly serve to determine whether a technical recovery or correction is about to occur or if the coming change in direction will turn out to be a trend reversal.

Specifics

In a bull market, when a market is overbought, the uptrend falters and may be followed by a technical correction.[3] After the technical correction, the market is oversold and the upotrend can begin again.

In a bear market, a market is oversold, the downtrend halts and may be followed by a price increase or a technical recovery.[4] When the technical recovery ends, the market is overbought and the downtrend will begin again.

In a bull market, the straight line between two successive highs is parallel to the straight line linking the two corresponding highs on the indicator. In a bear market, the straight line between two successive lows is parallel to the straight line linking the two corresponding lows on the indicator.

In the left-hand part of Figure 3.9, the 20-period moving average trend is downwards. The analysis will look only at the lows so as to predict which type of move (technical or a new trend) might occur.

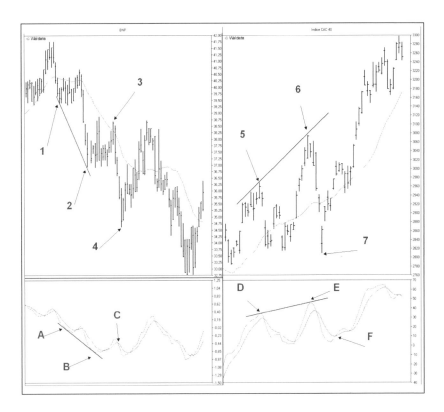

Figure 3.9   Overbought and oversold markets.

The straight line between lows 1 and 2 is parallel to that linking low points A and B. After point B a technical recovery is expected. This will have ended once the indicator is overbought at C, corresponding to high 3. After C, the main downtrend continues, towards a new low.

In the right-hand part of Figure 3.9, the main trend is up. The straight line between highs 5 and 6 is parallel to the straight line linking points D and E. In 6 we can see the start of a technical correction that ends when the market is oversold at F and at low 7. After F, the main uptrend takes off once more.

The dynamic approach

The smaller the time lag between an overbought/oversold state for a unit of time and the next unit of time up, the stronger the move.

Management

The criterion is weighted 40.

The basic rule is as follows: when the main trend is rising, as soon as the market is oversold, you can strengthen your position. If the market is overbought, you should leave your position unchanged.

When the main trend is down, as soon as the market is overbought, you can strengthen your position. If the market is oversold, you should leave your position unchanged.

On an hourly or sub-hourly chart, the weighting is 25% if you want to take a buy or sell position,[5] but you are not allowed to increase your position. On daily and longer units of time, the weighting for taking a position is 30%. You are allowed to strengthen your position once, applying a weighting of 25% of the criterion.

Divergence

A divergence signals a trend reversal. Divergences can be observed in a dynamic analysis of successive overbought and oversold states over a single unit of time. Both upward and downward divergences are found.

Definition

A downward divergence occurs in a market where the main trend is up. At the time of a high, a divergence appears between the straight line joining two consecutive price highs and that joining the indicator highs. The indicator's reversal level is lower than that of the previous reversal. The straight line joining the indicator highs slopes downwards, whereas the straight line joining price highs slopes upwards.

An upward divergence takes place in a market where the main trend is down. At the time of a new price low, we see convergence between the straight line joining two consecutive price lows and that joining the indicator floors.

When an upward divergence is observed on the major unit of time, any short positions taken out by the investor should be bought; you can take up a buy position.[6] When a downward divergence is observed on the major unit of time, any long positions must be sold; you can take a sell position.

The dynamic approach

A first approach looks at the biggest unit of time where the divergence is observed.

The first divergence is observed on the shortest unit of time. Then, gradually, divergences are observed on the next units of time up. Then, on a given unit of time, no further divergence is seen. Either an overbought/oversold market is seen, or no signs of a technical correction/recovery are evident. On a given market, the longest unit of time where the divergence was first identified allows you to define a framework for the scope of the expected movement by looking in the product's historic series for a similar divergence pattern.

If, following a divergence, no trend change is observed, this means that the longest unit of time where a divergence has occurred will be found on a longer unit of time.

A second approach involves comparing the measurement of the time between divergences or overbought/oversold states for a given unit of time and the next one up — for example, hourly and daily or principal and major.

An analysis of the historical series allows you to measure the scale of the expected change. The bigger the time gap, the less powerful the move.

In Figure 3.10, a bearish divergence can be seen at point B. The overbought state at B is below the previous one at A. The high 2 on

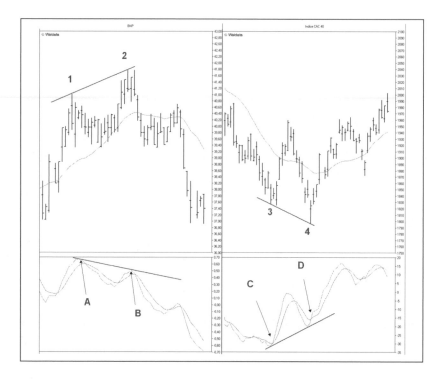

Figure 3.10   Bearish divergence and bullish divergence.

the stock price which corresponds to crossover B on the indicator is above the previous high at 1. The curve joining highs 1–2 diverges from curve A–B linking the indicator reversal points.

A bullish divergence emerges at point D. The oversold state at D is above that of the previous one at C. The price support at 4 corresponding to the crossover at D is below the previous low at 3 on the price line. The curve linking lows 3–4 converges with curve C–D linking the indicator's break-out points.

Management

The criterion's weighting is 85.

On a certain unit of time, you may see a divergence in either or both of these two indicators. If a divergence occurs only on the stochastic, the minimum scope of the movement will trigger an over-bought or oversold state on the next unit of time up. The weighting for this configuration is 70%. If the divergence occurs only on the MACD, the move will be a major one. A divergence on the stochastic of the next unit of time up is probable. The coefficient for this configuration is 110%. This is the strongest signal that one can observe. If a divergence is observed on the stochastic and on the MACD, the scope of the next move will not be weak. The weighting for this configuration is 100%. A divergence on the MACD of the next unit of time up should not be ruled out.

A word of caution about indicator representations

Many tests have shown that there are slight differences among software packages in the ways indicators are represented. I suggest that you calibrate your indicators using the parameters available in the software package in order to obtain curves as similar as possible to those shown here. In keeping with my devotion to the notion of safety, I have provided two charts (non-trending market, trending market) that you can use as benchmarks: see Figures 3.11 and 3.13.

Each of the indicators should take up 25% of the screen height. In terms of breadth, the start and closing prices must be visible on the bar chart. Furthermore, the size of the screen must allow you to see two resistance levels and two support levels so that you can detect divergences. As this comment is valid for all three units of time involved, this means that a 17-inch screen is necessary at the very least. Not only that, but using a smaller screen requires more sustained attention and over time this causes fatigue, which can translate into depleted concentration. A mistake will cost more than the price difference between a small screen and a big one.

Stochastic[7]

This is a very volatile indicator used by investors to analyse a market when the 20-period moving average is flat. The stochastic is also used by speculators, mainly as a safety aid.

Formula

The formula is calculated by subtracting the lowest low from the current close, dividing the difference by the difference between the highest high and the lowest low, and multiplying the quotient by 100.[8] The indicator is marked %K and its moving average %D.

Standard parameters

There is a so-called fast stochastic based on a moving average of 9 periods and a slow stochastic based on 14 periods. I always use the model based on 14 periods, while the moving averages cover 3 periods.

Optimization

To calculate %K and %D you are advised to use a modified moving average.

Calibration

The left-hand part of Figure 3.11 shows the stochastic in a strongly trending market. Note the non-crossover between the stochastic and its moving average at point A. The right-hand part of Figure 3.11 shows the stochastic when the market is flat.

Location on the chart

The stochastic is placed under the price line.

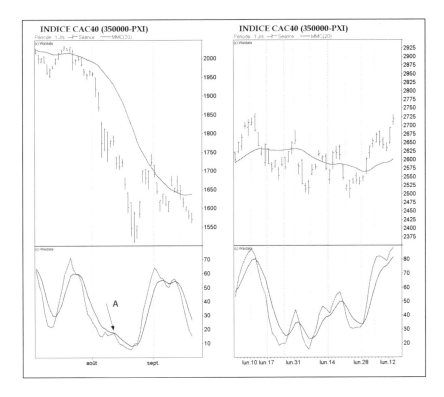

Figure 3.11 Calibrating the stochastic.

Reading the stochastic

Reading the stochastic consists of analysing the %K and %D curves. Did a crossover of the two curves trigger a divergence or simply an overbought/oversold state? If a reversal of %K occurred, what is or will be the type of crossover? Will a divergence on a lower unit of time spread to other units of time? Has a non-crossover just occurred? And so on.

On the left in Figure 3.12, the moving average is heading downwards. We analyse the lows. The market is oversold at A and B. The straight lines between 1 and 2 and between A and B are divergent. A

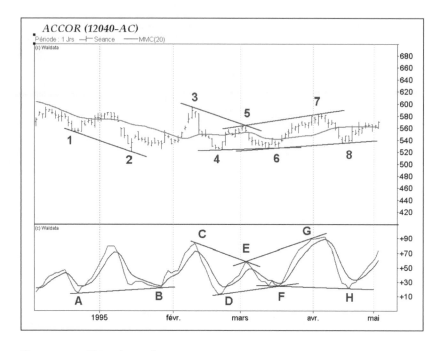

Figure 3.12 Using the stochastic.

trend reversal has begun at point B. From this point on, the trend should be bullish. However, the moving average has flattened, denoting a stable market. All the extremes must be analysed. The straight lines 3–5 and C–E are parallel. A technical correction has begun at point 5 and prices should not drop below their level at point 4. The straight line 4–6 is running parallel to the straight line D–F. From point 6 on, the bullish "micro" trend has picked up again. From point 7 onwards, we should reason in the same way as we did at point 5. At point H, the straight lines 6–8 and F–H are divergent. This is not a genuine divergence, however, because the low at point 8 should have been lower than point 6,while point H should not have been lower than point F.

When to observe the stochastic

When the moving average over 20 periods is flat, this is the most suitable (or least unsuitable) indicator for identifying trend reversals. You should observe the stochastic just before the end of the period of the major unit of time, so that you are ready if a crossover or a non-crossover is observed at the start of the following period.

In a strongly trending market, the stochastic is of no use as it is soon saturated. However, in markets like these, so long as they are neither overbought nor oversold, no other indicator is useful since there are no doubts about the ongoing trend.

Don'ts

Never base your decision on a reading of the stochastic. Remember that it is only a forward indicator whose signals must be borne out by those of the second indicator, the MACD.

Shortcomings

The volatility of this indicator generates a certain number of false signals in a flat market.

MACD

The MACD is the preferred indicator when the moving average over 20 periods is not stable. The existence of an overbought/oversold state on the major unit of time will allow you to start the order placing process.[9] But if the market starts to trend strongly, it will be saturated and will no longer be of any use.

Formula

The MACD represents the difference between two moving averages. Your software's on-line help will give you the formula.[10]

Standard parameters

I do not use the standard values of 26 and 12 to calculate the MACD, nor 9 for the average, as the time lag these trigger with the signals from the stochastic is too big.

Optimization

I think the values 19, 9 and 6 are most suitable, regardless of the unit of time involved.

Calibration

The left-hand part of Figure 3.13 shows how the indicator changes when the market is trendless. The right-hand part shows how the indicator moves when the market is trending strongly.

Location on the chart

The MACD is displayed beneath the stochastic.

Reading the MACD

Since the trend in Figure 3.14 is up, analysis of overbought states will be only carried out on the tops. The first top is point 1, when the

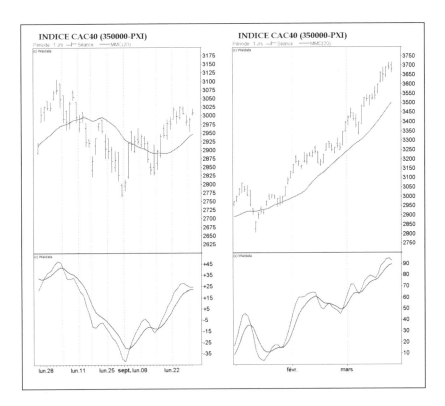

Figure 3.13   Calibrating the MACD.

MACD becomes overbought at point A. The straight line 1−2 is parallel to A−B. From point 2 onwards a technical correction is expected. After point 2, when the market is oversold at point C, the main uptrend picks up again. The market is now likely to overtop point 2.

The straight line 2−4 is diverging from B−D. A trend reversal thus took place at point 4. Prices are now expected to fall.

Figure 3.14   Stock prices and the MACD.

When to observe the MACD

As soon as the stochastic is overbought/oversold you have to start watching the MACD. Sometimes the crossovers take place simultaneously.

Don'ts

Don't anticipate a crossover until after the end of the period. Don't take the optimization signals you see on the lower unit of time into account.

Shortcomings

When it is used to unwind a position, the signals may not provide an appropriate result if the swing is substantial.

Simultaneous Use of Two Indicators

As a general rule, a signal from the stochastic means a short, narrow move. A signal from the MACD indicates a strong move.

If a crossover on the stochastic is not confirmed on the MACD, you should consider that in the short term the market will follow the trend shown by the most volatile indicator − the stochastic − and that in the longer term the market will track the trend shown by the MACD.

In Figure 3.15, the stochastic has crossed its moving average at point A. Two weeks later, at point B, the MACD has still not crossed its moving average. This situation heralds a small-scale technical correction. The underlying trend, shown by the MACD, is bullish. When, two weeks later, the MACD penetrates its moving average, the correction will have practically finished.

The Dynamic Approach

Table 3.1 summarizes the effects on the various units of time of a divergence or overbought/oversold state observed on the major unit of time. For a given unit of time, the shorter the time lag between a crossover on the stochastic and on the MACD, the stronger the move will be. Similarly, the shorter the period, for a given unit of time and the next unit of time up, between an overbought/oversold state or a divergence, the more powerful the move. Finally, the more a divergence is propagated on large-scale units of time, the stronger

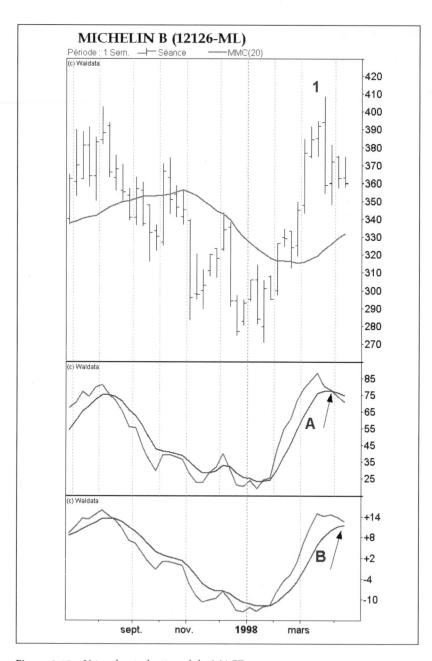

Figure 3.15 Using the stochastic and the MACD.

Table 3.1 Dynamic approach for the stochastic and MACD.

	Stochastic		MACD	
	Divergence[b]	Overbought–Oversold[c]	Divergence	Overbought–Oversold
Principal unit of time				
Stochastic	Divergence[b]	Overbought–Oversold[c]	Divergence	Overbought–Oversold
MACD	Divergence/Overbought–Oversold	Divergence/Overbought–Oversold/Nothing	Divergence/Overbought–Oversold	Overbought–Oversold/Nothing[d]
Major unit of time				
Stochastic	—	—	Divergence/Overbought–Oversold	Divergence/Overbought–Oversold
MACD	Divergence/Overbought–Oversold	Divergence/Overbought–Oversold	—	—
Control unit of time				
Stochastic	Divergence	Divergence/Overbought–Oversold	Divergence/Overbought–Oversold	Divergence/Overbought–Oversold
MACD	Divergence/Overbought–Oversold	Divergence/Overbought–Oversold	Divergence	Divergence/Overbought–Oversold

[a] Effect on the other units of time of different states of the major unit of time's stochastic and the MACD.
[b] Divergence may be bearish or bullish.
[c] Overbought–oversold state.
[d] Neither divergence nor overbought–oversold state.

the move will be. These are subjective observations, so you will consequently have to calibrate each market.

3.2. Target Indicators

The two indicators used are of the moving average type.[11] They allow you to determine upside and downside targets depending on their position in relation to prices. By using different triptychs, you can identify the objectives best suited to individual users. One of these indicators does, however, have another capital function: it allows you to determine the future state of the markets, and hence shows you which indicators to concentrate on. The 20-period moving average we have been using up to now as an indicator is a component of one of these two indicators I will now proceed to analyse. What is more, when the markets are trending strongly, target indicators become benchmark indicators in order to forecast market changes, whether the trader is an investor or a speculator.

These indicators, the parabolic and the Bollinger bands, are also used by speculators to take, manage and generally unwind their positions.

Parabolic

The parabolic is a very popular tool among currency traders. Generally used as a trend-change indicator in volatile markets, it also provides information when fluctuations are in a narrow range.

Use

The parabolic is used as a target for support and resistance levels by all traders.

Formula

The parabolic is a sort of exponential moving average. You will find the algorithm used to compute it in *New Concepts in Technical Trading Systems* (J. Welles Wilder Jr, Trend Research, 1978).

Standard parameters

The standard parameters are always applied.

Calibration

Differences in the value of the parabolic from one system to another and on the same unit of time are due to the length of the historical series used.[12]

The left-hand part of Figure 3.16 shows changes to the parabolic (the dotted curve) in a strongly trending market. The right-hand part shows the parabolic in a weakly trending market.

Optimization

None.

Indicator identification in DTAFM^R

The parabolic is represented by the letter P.

Location on the chart

On the price line in the shape of a series of dots forming a curve.

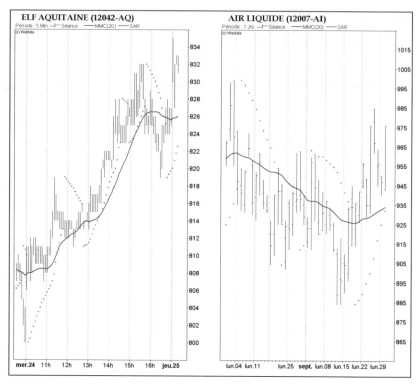

Figure 3.16   Calibrating the parabolic.

Reading the parabolic

When the parabolic is above the price line, the market is bearish. When below, it is bullish. During a given period, prices touching or crossing the parabolic signal a trend change.

The shape of the curve formed by a succession of values also provides information. You can draw a straight line from the first two points. The flatter and longer the line, the weaker the ongoing trend. This shows a technical movement. Conversely, if the straight line is at an angle and takes the shape of a parabolic curve, or if, after a number of periods, the points move away from the curve formed by the first two points, this signals a strong trend.

When you see a crossover of the indicator and the market, the parabolic will take the value of the previous top/bottom in the next period. You will see a break in the curve whenever a trend change is signalled.

At 1 in Figure 3.17, the points form a flat, straight line. The ongoing downward movement is no more than a technical correction. After 2, the points diverge from the straight line formed by the first three points. This signals the start of an uptrend. It will not be called into doubt when prices move below it. Note that the curve formed after point 3 is steeper than the one starting at 2. The price increase that takes place from 3 is bigger than the one that began after 2. From time to time, we may not observe a plateau phase at the

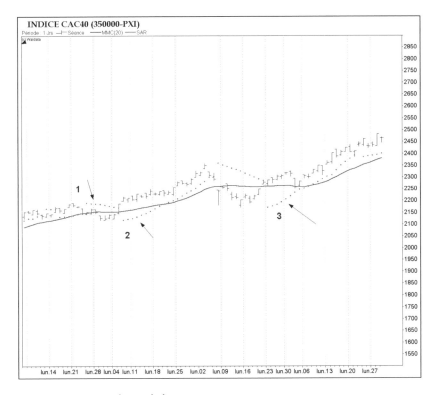

Figure 3.17 Using the parabolic.

outset. The first points form a sloping straight line. In this case, the move may be very strong. On the other hand, the longer the straight line remains flat, the less chance we have of seeing a strong move.

When to observe the parabolic

At all times, since as soon as the parabolic is touched or crossed by the price, we see a trend reversal. If not, the parabolic's value remains unchanged over a period of time. Moreover, the algorithm gives you the value of the next period's parabolic, although this will assume the value of the previous top if prices cross the indicator.

Don'ts

Don't anticipate a crossover of the parabolic and prices. If the parabolic is approached without being crossed, this means that a large-scale trend reversal is in the offing. On the other hand, if prices cross the parabolic, you should expect to see an amplification of the trend during the ongoing and subsequent periods.

Shortcomings

The parabolic must not be analysed in isolation.

On non-organized markets, price mistakes in databases can have a large-scale impact on the behaviour of the indicator.

The dynamic approach

There is no correlation between the various units of time, so dynamic analysis is meaningless. In Figure 3.18, note the strong uptrend in the parabolics on the major and control units of time, whereas the parabolic is moving down on the principal unit of time.

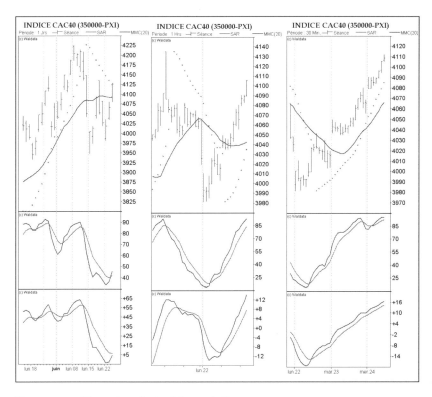

Figure 3.18 Dynamic analysis of the parabolic.

Bollinger Bands

Bollinger bands are a group of three curves (the upper band, the moving average and the lower band) which, depending on their position in relation to prices, are used as support and resistance levels by investors and speculators. The shapes formed by the bands help you forecast the type of state the market is likely to show. This is the speculator's favourite model. Investors use Bollinger bands to unwind their positions when prices trend strongly, because it is currently the best model for taking advantage of strong volatility and price variations. As this is a model based on a statistical law, it is equally effective on a chart with a one-minute unit of time and on one with a one-month unit of time. Furthermore, the validity of the model will not be challenged regardless of the number of users. In practice, Bollinger bands are never used without the parabolic.

Formula

The three curves are: a 20-period moving average called the Bollinger moving average; the upper Bollinger band, which is equivalent to the moving average plus two standard deviations; and the lower Bollinger band, which is equivalent to the Bollinger moving average minus two standard deviations. See your software's on-line help facility for further details.

Commentary

The 20-period moving average used since the start of the book is close to Bollinger's moving average computed using an average price range (highest + lowest + period close divided by 3) instead of just the closing price. From this point on, therefore, the 20-period moving average will be displayed as a Bollinger moving average.

Standard parameters

It is usual to observe two standard deviations, because 95% of all prices will be expected to fall between the upper and lower Bollinger bands.

Calibration

The left-hand part of Figure 3.19 shows Bollinger bands in a bullish market, while the right-hand part shows Bollinger bands in a weakly trending market.

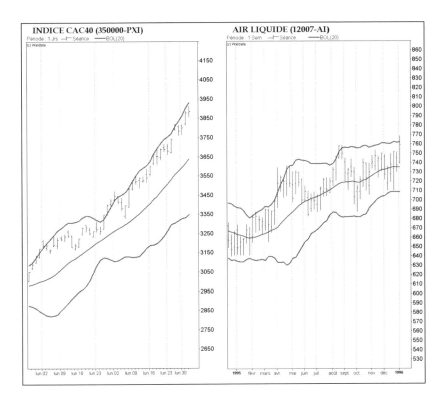

Figure 3.19 Calibrating Bollinger bands.

Optimization

None.

Location on the chart

Like the parabolic, Bollinger bands are placed on either side of the price line.

Identification in DTAFM®

Upper Bollinger band: U.
Lower Bollinger band: L.
Bollinger moving average: M.

Don'ts

Don't restrict yourself to reading curves on the major unit of time. Don't concentrate on reading the control unit of time.

Reading the Bollinger bands

Stable market on the major unit of time

The Bollinger bands and the moving average are both flat. Prices fluctuate between the upper and lower bands. The stochastic reverses when one of the bands, U or L, is touched. The parabolic is flat and may be found above or below the Bollinger moving average. If the stochastic becomes overbought/oversold near the parabolic/Bollinger moving average zone, there is a strong probability that prices are about to start trending. When tracking a stable market, only the stochastic is used. It is generally difficult to make money in a market like this. I do not recommend taking a position when confronted with such configurations.

In Figure 3.20, the Bollinger bands and moving average are both flatlining. The stochastic is the most suitable indicator for tracking price fluctuations.

When the stochastic is overbought (A, C and E), prices have risen and the upper Bollinger band serves as a resistance level (1, 3, 5). When the stochastic is oversold (B and D), prices have fallen and the lower band serves as a support level (2, 4).

The semi-bubble is a chart that goes with the stable market, and will be presented later in the book.

Weakly trending market

The Bollinger moving average on the major unit of time is slightly biased up or down. The Bollinger bands are wide apart and more or less parallel but do not form any specific configuration. The Bollinger bands serve as support and resistance levels. If prices close outside the Bollinger bands at a given point, the previous period's top will

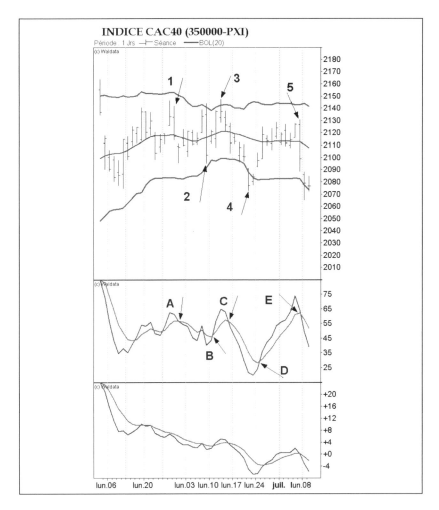

Figure 3.20 Stable market.

not be overtopped during the next period. The MACD is the most suitable indicator for tracking the market when it is in this state. Investors may take a position in this configuration if they observe the rules set out in the MACD analysis.

On the price line in Figure 3.21, the Bollinger moving average is not flatlining. The MACD is the most suitable indicator for tracking

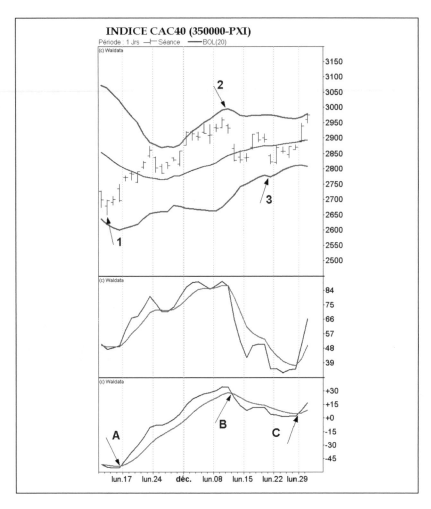

Figure 3.21 Weakly trending market.

price swings. When the MACD is oversold (A) prices move from the lower Bollinger band 1 towards the upper band 2, at which point the MACD is overbought (B). The Bollinger band serves as a resistance level and prices move towards the lower band at 3. Notice that only one closing price takes place outside the upper Bollinger band.

Strongly trending market

Prices move outside the Bollinger bands for several successive periods and the Bollinger moving average is strongly bullish or strongly bearish. The curve formed by the parabolic also shows a trend.

At point 1 in Figure 3.22, prices close outside the upper Bollinger band and at point 2 break out from the top at 1, despite the fact that the stochastic is not overbought. Parallel curves can be observed. At point A on the MACD note a non-crossover that indicated strengthening bullish potential on the MACD. Subsequently, the position purchased at point 2 will be partly unwound at point 3 and partly at point 4.

All the indicators have now been presented.

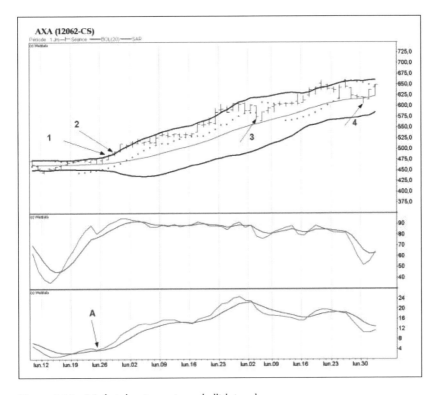

Figure 3.22 Market showing a strong bullish trend.

Large-scale price swings generally occur when prices break out of a Bollinger band. In this case, various specific configurations are formed by the Bollinger bands. These should be analysed, because they are used by all traders to manage their positions and generate large capital gains.

Notes

1. Note that this is in respect of DTAFM® criteria. Paragraphs devoted to management can be skipped at first reading.
2. This information is given simply to enable readers to compare the importance of the various criteria. Each criterion is weighted out of 100, where 100 represents the least risky pattern (identification of parallels on the lower unit of time) or a full position (say, buy 100 shares). Depending on their needs, traders can modify the weightings of criteria. To do this, you need to have mastered DTAFM® completely, which will take several weeks' practice.
3. When the main trend is bullish, a limited downward move may occur.
4. When the main trend is bearish, a limited upward move may occur.
5. This position is taken following the appearance of a signal on the next unit of time up, and by confirmation on the next unit of time down.
6. See the necessary conditions in Section 2.3, and other conditions to be presented later.
7. See George C. Lane, "Lane Stochastics", *Technical Analysis of Stocks and Commodities*, May/June 1984.
8. Ibid.
9. See the conditions mentioned in Section 2.3.
10. Gerald Appel, Signalert Corporation, Great Neck, NY 11021, USA.
11. The way I use these indicators will horrify statisticians. I am perfectly aware of the mistakes committed from a theoretical point of view.
12. The value to use is the one obtained by taking account of the complete historical series in the database.

Chapter 4

Strongly Trending Market: Parallels and Bubble

Speculators can make substantial capital gains with a minimum of risk when certain configurations are probable. The upstream signals are sufficiently characteristic to allow them to take a position before the new trend starts and to exit the market when it is nearing its end. That means it is easy to seek opportunities by calling up on a triptych the database of the markets where they want to trade. Among the securities they analyse, it is not unusual to find one or two perfect profiles on which they can trade and make a substantial capital gain.

A position taken by investors can also change very suddenly. Their appreciation of the risks they are running will allow them to act accordingly.

When prices break out of the Bollinger bands, the bands form a family of patterns variously dubbed parallels, bubbles and semi-bubbles. The relationships between parallels and bubbles are comparable to those which exist between a divergence and an overbought/oversold state. Parallels change into bubbles in the next unit of time up. Parallels appear spontaneously on a given unit of time when a divergence propagates from the smallest unit of time to another, higher, unit of time. Conversely, just as the transition from divergence to an overbought/oversold state on a greater unit of time points to the longest unit of time where the movement occurs, the transition from parallels to a bubble also signals a peak in the propagation of the move's strength. In the case of parallels, however, it is possible that parallel curves might reappear two or three units of time up.

Parallels and bubbles are patterns which have a shared component. The figures can be broken down into several distinct phases:

Phase 1: initialization
Phase 2: confirmation
Phase 3: acceleration
Phase 4: bubbles and parallels
Phase 5: end of parallels and bubbles.

Differentiation only takes place after phase 3. Semi-bubbles are a variant on bubbles.

Observing rules concerning position-taking sometimes leads to shortfalls because no position has been taken. At other times, the position you have taken has to be closed, despite the possibility of a substantial gain if the position had been kept open. However, you should never regret a missed trade; and, above all, never take a position at a time different from that indicated.

In the rest of this chapter we look at the criteria needed for figure formation.

4.1. Phase 1: Initialization

For speculators, this phase can only be considered to exist in a market where the Bollinger bands and the Bollinger moving average have been flat for six periods or more.

T0 begins at the time of the last close inside the Bollinger bands when prices touch (but do not cross) the upper Bollinger band if the stochastic is not overbought, or at the time of the last close inside the Bollinger bands when prices touch (without crossing) the lower band, if the stochastic is not oversold.

During the following period, prices must cross the closest Bollinger band. A gap[1] is often observed here, marking the start of the T1 period. Furthermore, the essential thing is to observe a closing price outside the upper or lower band at the end of the period during which a Bollinger band has been crossed. It is also necessary to have seen an acceleration[2] during this same period. Moreover, the Bollinger bands must be diverging and the parabolic and the Bollinger moving average must be trending.

The more perfectly symmetrical the Bollinger bands, the more powerful the trend. This point is very important. Similarly, the longer the symmetry lasts, the sharper the trend.

Another vital point to consider before moving on to explore the parallels is the distance between the Bollinger bands. The longer the stable phase before the market starts trending, the narrower the distance between the bands (low market volatility). Beyond six periods of stability, it is unusual to see any problems of distance between the bands. If the number of periods of stable prices is less than 6, on the other hand, or if the market has reversed from a bullish to a bearish trend or vice versa, you should check the recent historic series to make sure that parallels have already been formed in the present context of the distance between the bands in view of current market volatility, prices and Bollinger bands. The issue is especially important when a parallel configuration ends. Beginners are advised not to take a position to take advantage of parallels that are moving in the opposite direction from those observed in recent periods when this configuration is visible without a prior plateau phase, because in most cases these are not real parallels forming and the outcome is rarely positive. It is better not to take a position if the bands seem too wide apart.[3]

At T1 in Figure 4.1, prices have closed outside the upper Bollinger band. Subsequently, however, the price rises were limited. You can see that between low point 1 and T1, prices have risen sharply. Yet before the start of the new trend, the Bollinger bands were in a downward parallel configuration where position-taking was not permitted.

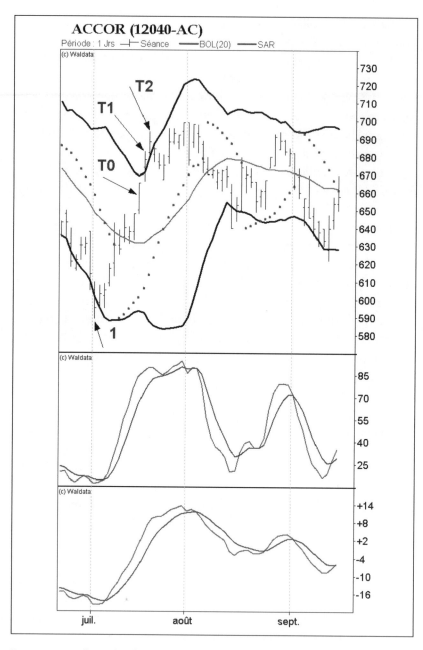

Figure 4.1   Bollinger bands too wide apart.

Calibration

If we are to analyse a divergence correctly, the distance between two bar charts must be neither too small nor too great. The same distance between two bar charts must be used on all three charts in the triptych.[4] Use Figure 4.2 to calibrate your screen.

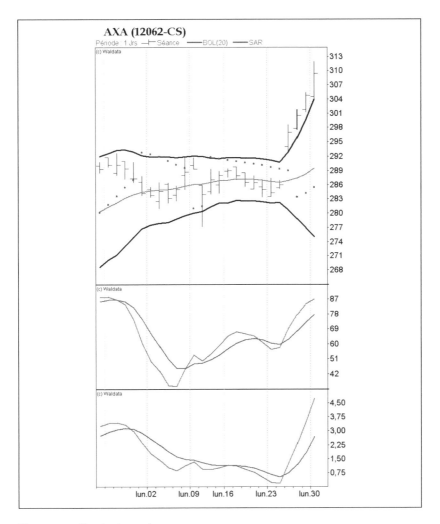

Figure 4.2   Bar chart spread.

Benchmark

An analysis of the historical series of Bollinger band divergence will help you assess the strength of the trend. In your early trades, select the trends which most resemble those in Figure 4.3. There, all the criteria are present during period T1: there is a stable phase lasting more than six periods with flat Bollinger bands; the gap between the Bollinger bands was relatively narrow in the previous periods; the gap has appeared, so that prices can break out of the upper Bollinger band; the stochastic is not overbought; and there is an acceleration between opening and closing prices and a symmetrical divergence of the Bollinger bands.

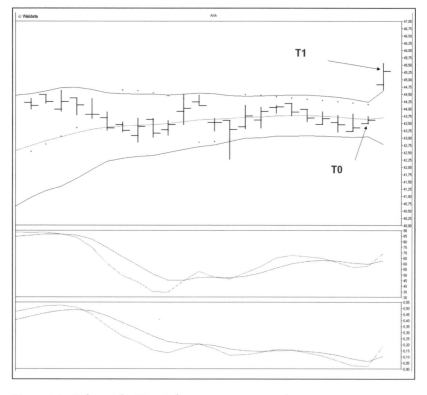

Figure 4.3   Reference for T1 period.

4.2. Phase 2: Confirmation

Start of Acceleration

If the top of period T1 is exceeded by three ticks[5] during the following period, speculators will always take out a position at that precise moment. We call this period T2 because parallels are forming. When this configuration occurs, investors who have had an open position since the MACD on the control unit of time signalled them to do so will close out their positions, as will speculators.

In Figure 4.4, the conditions exist during T2 to take a position as soon as the high in T1 has been exceeded by three ticks.

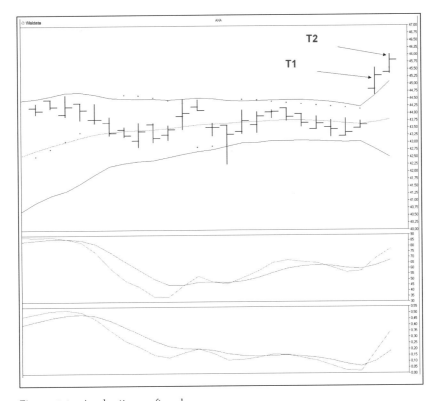

Figure 4.4 Acceleration confirmed.

Extreme Case of Acceleration

If the previous T1 period high is touched without being crossed, traders will take out a position at the start of the following period if prices closed outside the Bollinger bands. If not, speculators are not advised to take out a position.

In Figure 4.5, at T0, prices did not close outside the upper Bollinger band and the divergence of the Bollinger bands is not

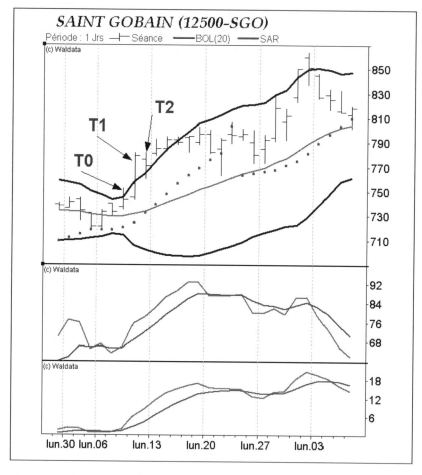

Figure 4.5   Extreme case of acceleration.

convincing. On the other hand, at T1, an acceleration between opening and closing prices is discernible, and this takes place a long way from the Bollinger band. No acceleration is visible at T2, and the period high is the same as in the previous period. Because the close was outside the Bollinger band, speculators will take out positions at the start of the following period.

Non-conforming Configuration

You must never take out a position when conditions are not right. In Figure 4.6, at both T1 and T2, prices have not managed to close outside the lower Bollinger band. More serious things are taking place at T1, however, in the form of a non-acceleration is clearly discernible. At T2, the gap between the opening and closing prices is also too narrow to talk of an acceleration. The first acceleration at T3 takes place too late to take out a position.

At T1 in Figure 4.7, the closing price is too similar to the opening price for us to speak of an acceleration. What is more, at T2, the highest price is lower than the top at T1. There are no upwardly mobile parallels and the next period must not be identified as T2. Speculators must not take out a position. Investors, on the other hand, will maintain their position as indicated earlier.

Lack of Confirmation

At T2, if the top of the preceding T1 period is not reached, there are no parallels. Investors will close out their position using the MACD.

The situation in Figure 4.8 is worse than in the preceding one. After opening on a high, prices fall continually during period T1, as they do in T2. There are no possible parallels. The bar charts outside the Bollinger bands must not be marked T1 and T2.

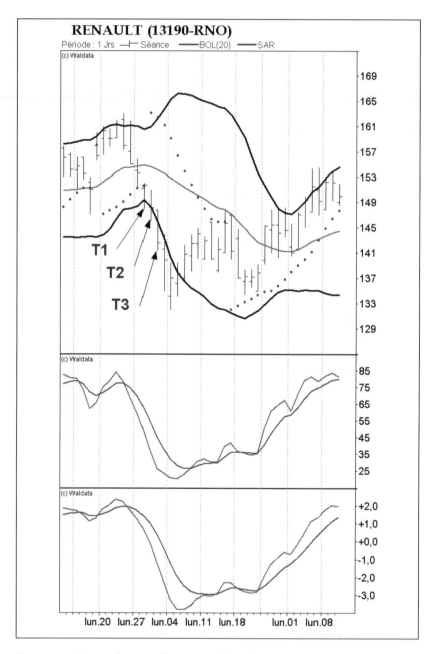

Figure 4.6   Non-conformity with situation observed at T2.

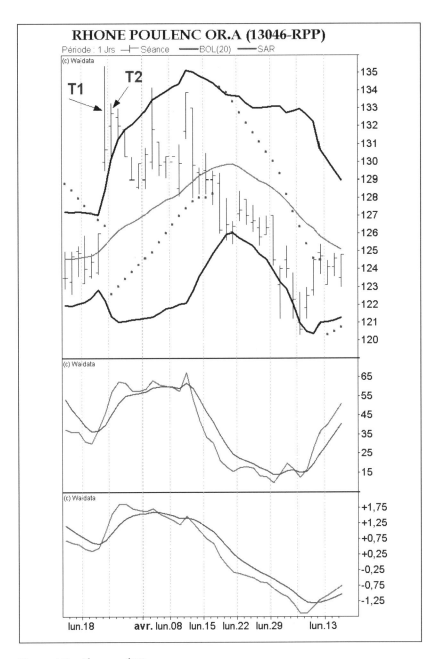

Figure 4.7   Absence of T2.

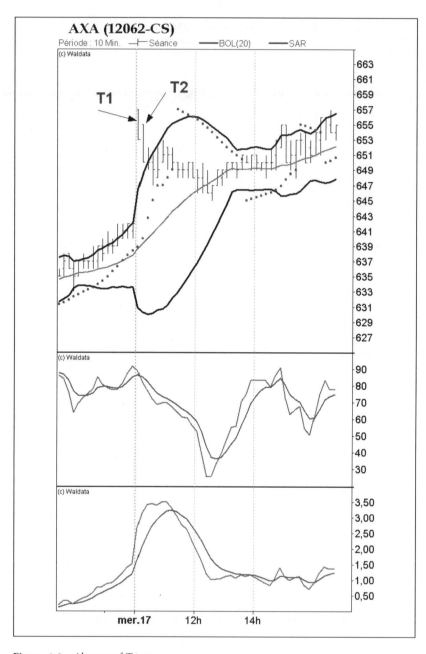

Figure 4.8   Absence of T1.

Controlling the Position

During periods T2, T3 and T4 of the major unit of time, if the control unit of time is hourly or sub-hourly, you must close out the position if the opposite Bollinger band of the control unit of time is crossed.

If the control unit of time is daily or weekly, the position will be unwound if the control unit of time's Bollinger moving average is crossed. Similarly, if a divergence of the stochastic or the MACD is observed on the control unit of time, you must close out the position. If the acceleration falters, you must keep an eye on the opposing Bollinger band. If this retains a trend symmetrical with the other, and if the position is still a winning one, there is no reason to move. If the opposite band stagnates, the chart shows a semi-bubble. I shall be analysing this case below. If the gains are cancelled out, you must liquidate the position on the basis of signals from the control unit of time.

At T1 and T2 in the left-hand part of Figure 4.9, the situation is normal. At T3, however, a downward gap occurs. The price has fallen below the purchase price, and on the next unit of time down the price crosses the parabolic. During T4, when the moving average on the control unit of time is crossed, speculators must close out their positions. Investors have no reason to close out their buyer position taken in B when the oversold state of the daily MACD confirms the oversold state at A on the weekly unit of time. The next target is the opposite Bollinger band. Once the parabolic and the Bollinger moving average have been crossed, it is rare for the trend not to continue as far as the opposite Bollinger band.

When using hourly and sub-hourly units of time you should be extremely cautious, because price fluctuations can be very rapid.

4.3. Phase 3: Acceleration

At this stage, you will need to think about the potential strength of the ongoing trend. In 90% of cases, the choice will be limited to two

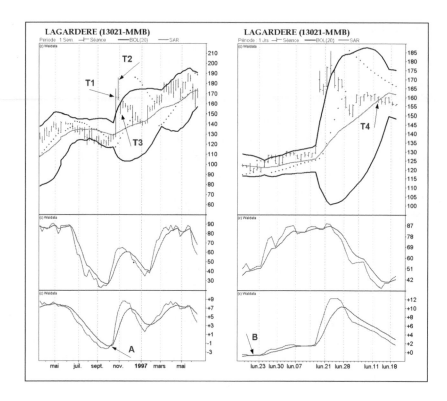

Figure 4.9 Safety.

configurations: parallels and the bubble. Depending on the type of pattern, you should be able to distinguish between a fast, brusque movement (the bubble) and a longer-lasting movement (parallels).

Anticipating the Type of Pattern

If, after breaking out of the Bollinger band, during the subsequent periods prices very soon start tracking the closest Bollinger band, there is a strong probability of seeing parallels. Often at T1 and at

T2 the close occurs near the Bollinger band then prices shadow or straddle the Bollinger band. When the parabolic crosses over the Bollinger moving average at the same time as the Bollinger bands continue to move apart, the expected figure is of the parallel type.

If, during the period following the crossover between the parabolic and the moving average, the furthest point in the previous period (a top in a bullish market or a bottom in a bearish) is exceeded, there is a strong probability of seeing parallels form. When the parabolic crosses the Bollinger moving average with a divergence between the upper band and the lower band, the pattern is assimilated to parallels.

If prices continue to edge away from the Bollinger band, the most probable hypothesis is a bubble.

In Figure 4.10, parallel bands are shown on the left-hand chart. At T1, the closing price is outside the upper Bollinger band. At T2 the expected acceleration occurs and continues through T3 and T4. Notice that prices shadow the upper Bollinger band pretty closely. On the opposite band you can see a V-shape, corresponding to the lack of a plateau phase. The right-hand chart shows a bubble. An acceleration has occurred at T1 and closing prices have broken out of the upper Bollinger band. From T2 to T4, prices move away from the upper Bollinger band, however. At T4, we see the opposite Bollinger band stabilizing, which marks the start of a plateau phase. After a correction, prices cannot get back into contact with the upper Bollinger band.

Safety

When prices have broken through the Bollinger bands, you hold on to the position so long as the stochastic is not overbought (bullish market) or oversold (bearish market). An overbought/oversold stochastic implies a need to close out the position. This situation is

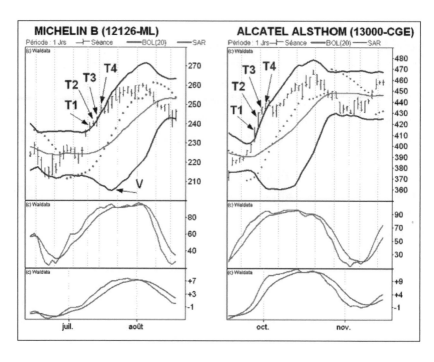

Figure 4.10   Parallels and bubble.

rare. You will encounter it in cases where the conditions for finding parallels on the major unit of time have not been met or if the opposite band on the next unit of time down has been crossed.

4.4. Phase 4: Bubble and Parallels

Existing Plateau Phase: Bubble

If the opposite Bollinger band stabilizes, a plateau phase of variable duration begins. When prices return within the Bollinger bands, the position is unwound, either when the stochastic is overbought/oversold, or when the plateau phase ends. This latter condition occurs in an overwhelming majority of cases.

In Figure 4.11, the position taken during the period following A, when the previous high has been strictly exceeded, is sold when the opposite band has reversed at B. Note that the stochastic is not yet overbought. The stochastic would have been used to close out the position if the overbought state had occurred before the end of the plateau phase. In the absence of a plateau phase, the rules for managing parallels would have applied.

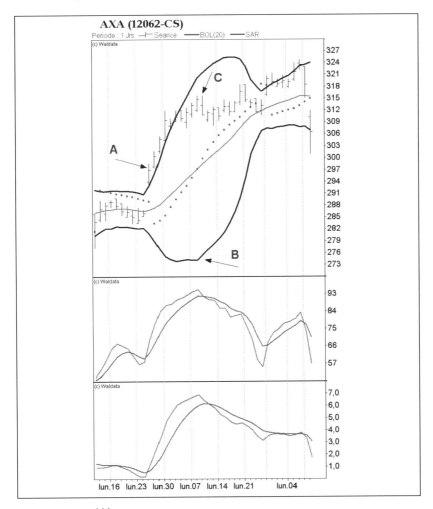

Figure 4.11   Bubble.

No Plateau or Plateau Embryonic: Parallels

In cases where the plateau phase does not occur, or is limited to three periods, the chart forms parallels. You will keep your position open so long as prices cross neither the parabolic nor the Bollinger moving

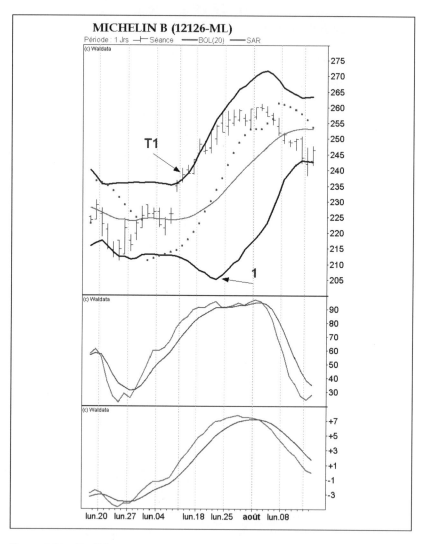

Figure 4.12   Parallels.

average. The longer the plateau phase, the more the probability of a bubble occurring increases. When no price correction occurs as the parabolic crosses over the Bollinger moving average, this indicates reserves of power in the market, qualifying the existence of parallels for this pattern.

At T1, in Figure 4.12, we note an acceleration, although it is not very sharp. Over subsequent periods, prices shadow the Bollinger band, heralding parallels. Perfect symmetry over a great number of periods points to the notion of parallels.

4.5. Phase 5: End of Parallels and Bubbles

The criteria for coming out of parallels and bubbles are different.

Parallels

The position is closed out in two stages. Fifty per cent of the position is unwound when the first of the two indicators (either the Bollinger moving average or the parabolic) is crossed, while the balance is sold off when the other indicator crosses over in turn. Note that the closing-out order is effective as soon as the parabolic is crossed. When it comes to the crossover between prices and the moving average, you can postpone half of the order so long as the crossover does not involve the closing price. I do, however, advise beginners not to use this latter option.

In Figure 4.13, 50% of the position is sold at point 1 when prices cross over the parabolic. In most cases, the parabolic is first to be crossed. The remaining 50% are sold when prices exceed the moving average at point 2. We were careful to split the closing of the transaction because in half of all cases, the moving average is crossed very soon after the parabolic.

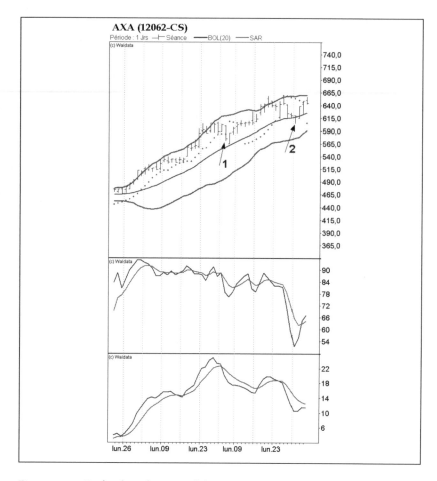

Figure 4.13 Profit-taking during parallels.

Bubbles

The position is unwound when the opposite band has reversed direction. At the point where this change takes place, we find a maximum number of prices in a bullish market, and a minimum in a bearish market. However, the reversal of this band is sometimes hard to spot, in which case the stochastic is used as a precautionary measure. In a bullish market an overbought stochastic tells you that the curve has already reversed. In a bearish market, an oversold stochastic indicates that the opposite band has effectively reversed.

The curve has reversed at point 1 in Figure 4.14. On the price line, level 2 corresponds to an acceptable point of sale. On the stochastic, the overbought state at A occurs during the period following point 1.

After the end of a bubble or parallels, three different shapes can evolve: a bubble (parallels) symmetrical to the previous one, a bubble (parallels) similar to the previous one, or flat Bollinger bands. As it is impossible to predict the type of figure, all positions must be unwound at the end of the bubble and of parallels.

The cases described above are met with frequently, so it is possible to restrict the use of DTAFM® to the notions I have just described

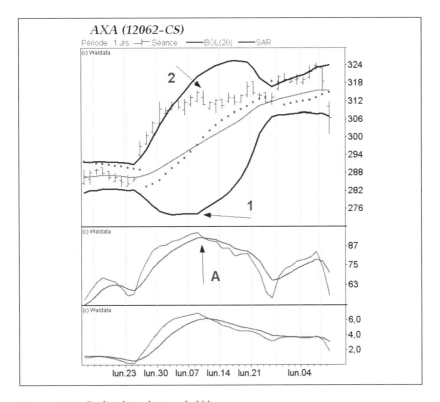

Figure 4.14   Profit-taking during a bubble.

and achieve a profit on nearly 90% of your trades. In practice, however, traders seek to get more out of the method because, although the situations I have just described are met with regularly, other configurations exist. These are variations on the theme of those just described. A presentation of these classic situations will help you exercise greater control over probable market moves and consequently trade more often.

Notes

1. An empty space between two bar charts.
2. Acceleration takes place if the gap between the opening and closing prices is the widest possible. In a bullish market, the opening price is as close as possible to the current low and the closing price as close as possible to the current high. In a bearish market, the start must be as close as possible to the current high and the closing price as close as possible to the current low. There should not be too sharp an acceleration at the outset to enable it to continue.
3. The default setting of commercial software is the space available in a window. With respect to the distance between the bands, this can lead to errors. It is often necessary to increase the length of the historic series in the window to get a more objective idea of the situation.
4. For presentational reasons, I have not always observed this rule here.
5. The tick is the smallest change permitted in the price of a futures contract.

Chapter 5

Aids to Analysis

The points presented in this chapter are independent of each other and the only relation between them is that they are regularly seen in the charts. If investors and speculators take them into account, they will shorten the learning phase by several months and be operational that much faster.

5.1. Reclassifying a Bubble as Parallels

Non-crossover on the Stochastic

When a non-crossover appears on the stochastic before the end of the plateau phase, the bubble changes to a parallel configuration. The rules for unwinding parallels apply.

In Figure 5.1, a plateau phase has existed on the opposite band since point 2. The speculator will wait either for the end of the plateau phase, or for an oversold state, before repurchasing the position sold at point 1. The non-crossover seen at A on the stochastic changes the criteria governing profit-taking because the non-crossover during the plateau phase means we can qualify the chart as parallels. The management rules governing profit-taking on parallels therefore apply.

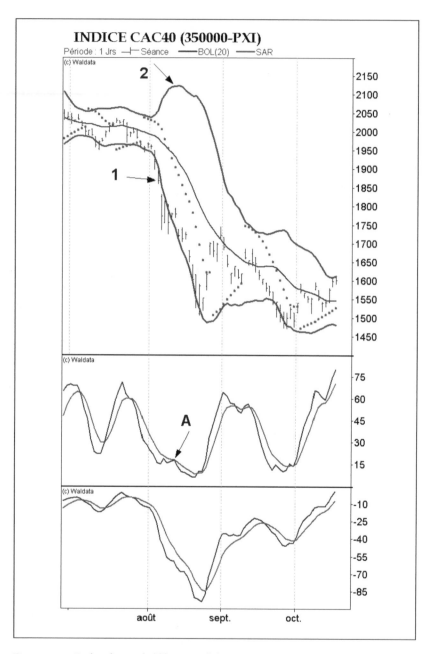

Figure 5.1   Reclassifying a bubble as parallels.

Impact of a Crossover between the Parabolic and the Bollinger Moving Average

When the parabolic crosses the Bollinger moving average, this means a market correction/technical recovery is starting or is already under way. But if you cannot see a trend reversal, this indicates considerable reserves of strength in the market and the expected figure is of the parallels type. We could even expect an acceleration of the ongoing trend during the following periods.

Continuation of trend

If the trend observed before the crossover between the parabolic and the Bollinger moving average continues during the period following the one after the crossover, traders who do not have open positions can take advantage of this opportunity to buy into the market. The situation is managed as if we had a pattern of parallels.

In Figure 5.2, the parabolic crosses the Bollinger moving average. During the following period, a new price high is observed at 1. Traders who do not have a position can enter the market during the subsequent period when there is a strong probability of seeing a close higher than the previous one. The position is managed as if the pattern were of the parallel type. Sell 50% of the position at the time of the crossover between the price and the parabolic (2). The remainder is closed out in two trades, when the price crosses the Bollinger moving average.

Correction/technical recovery not reaching the parabolic and the moving average

In a bullish market, during the correction (technical recovery) following the crossover between the parabolic and the Bollinger moving average, at each period a new low/high is observed. At the top/ bottom, if the parabolic has not been crossed, the previous bullish/ bearish trend will continue powerfully and make it worthwhile to

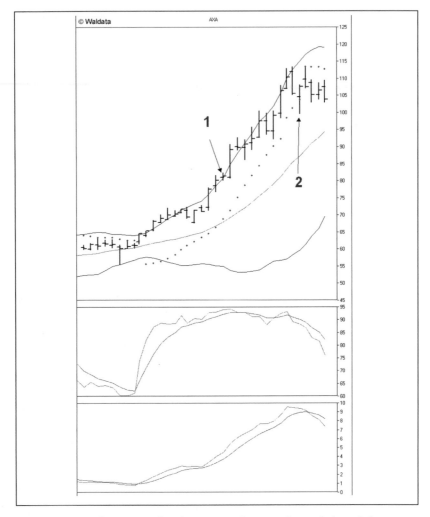

Figure 5.2   Trend continues after the crossover between the parabolic and the moving average.

take out a new position, as the current pattern is treated as parallels and the position will be managed as such.

In Figure 5.3, we have a purchase at point T2. After the crossover between the parabolic and the Bollinger moving average at point 1, a correction moving towards the parabolic is expected. But the fall

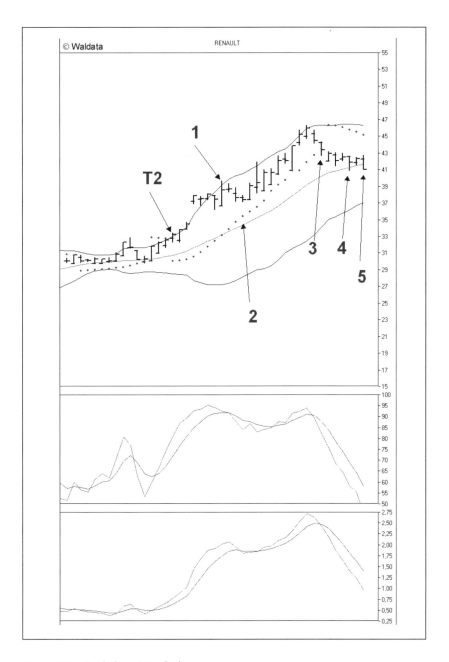

Figure 5.3 Parabolic not touched.

does not gather momentum. At point 2, the price approaches the parabolic without touching it. A purchase signal appears during the following period as soon as there is a probability that the closing price will break out beyond the top in the previous period. Fifty per cent of the position is sold at point 3 at the time of the crossover

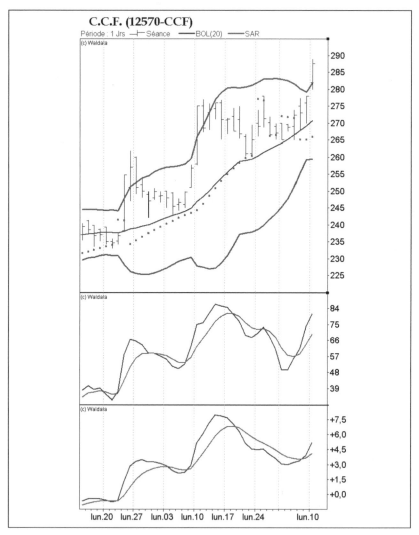

Figure 5.4   Non-crossover between the parabolic and the Bollinger moving average.

between the price and the parabolic. The remainder is closed out in two trades, when the price crosses the Bollinger moving average, points 4 and 5.

Non-crossover between the Parabolic and the Bollinger Moving Average

If no crossover between the parabolic and the Bollinger moving average has been noted before the trend reversal on the opposite band, the chart will be considered to show parallels and will be treated as such.

When the type of figure shown in Figure 5.4 is observed, 50% of the position is unwound by the speculator when the parabolic is crossed and the remaining 50% sold when the Bollinger moving average is crossed in due course. Note that on the chart, prices continue to rise, despite the fact that the MACD has been over-bought for some time.

5.2. Specific Features of Parallels

What Not to Do with Parallels

Do not postpone until point T3 or subsequently unwind prematurely if the trade goes into loss. If in doubt, don't opt for parallels. Don't interpret the instructions related to acceleration signals in phases T0 to T2.

A very frequent case you must constantly bear in mind is where, on the next unit of time up, the Bollinger bands are far apart. In this case, the parallels do not generate a bubble on the next unit of time up. As they approach the Bollinger band due to be crossed, prices are no longer in the acceleration phase (comparison of opening and closing prices) and the Bollinger band is used as a resistance or support level.

In Figure 5.5, the bands are so far apart at the start of the parallels that even if they show a gap occurring, they do not lead to an acceleration in the subsequent period.

Different Types of Parallels

Usable parallels

Prices break out of the Bollinger band at point T1 and close outside the bands. At point T2, the high of the previous period is exceeded by at least three ticks. During the subsequent periods prices shadow the Bollinger band closely.

Parallels that cannot be used by speculators

It may happen that prices may regularly shadow the Bollinger bands without any signal leading to an acceleration and by a closing break-out. However, after the opposite Bollinger band has reversed, the band nearest the price line does not change its trend and prices continue to shadow it closely. Although the pattern in Figure 5.6 looks like parallels, it does not necessarily possess their strength. This means that a semi-bubble may be generated on the principal unit of time. Investors will have taken a position before this figure has been detected and will hold it until the criteria for unwinding parallels can be applied. Speculators will only enter the market if the criteria enabling the bubble to be reclassified as parallels are met.

In the left-hand part of Figure 5.6, prices have closed outside the upper Bollinger band at point T1. The acceleration is confirmed at T2 and the speculator takes a buy position. Prices are tracking the upper Bollinger band. At point 1, the opposite Bollinger band reverses, with no prior plateau phase. The figure shows a parallels pattern. During the subsequent correction, 50% of the position is closed out at point 2

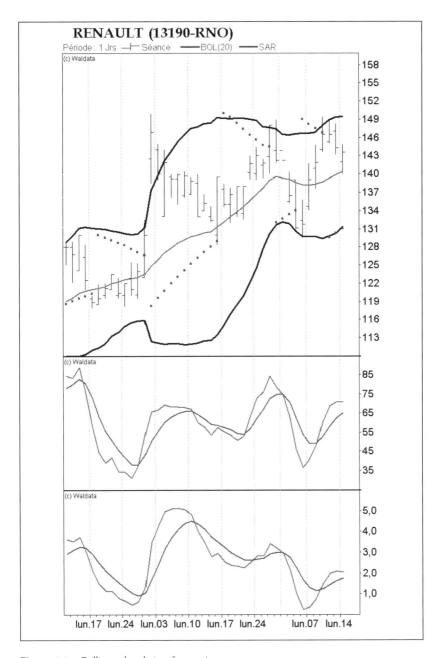

Figure 5.5 Bollinger bands too far apart.

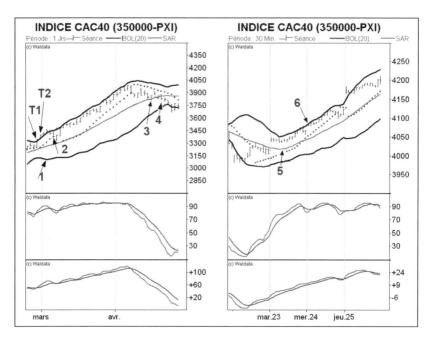

Figure 5.6   Usable and non-usable parallels for speculators.

when the price crosses the parabolic. Half of the remainder is sold when the Bollinger moving average is crossed on the downtrend at point 3. The rest is sold at point 4 when the closing price crosses the Bollinger moving average.

At point 5 in the right-hand part of Figure 5.6, the Bollinger moving average begins an uptrend. But although prices are rising, they are unable to cross the upper Bollinger band. From point 6 onwards, investors will apply the management criteria for parallels to unwind their positions, since prices have not crossed the parabolic after the crossover between the parabolic and the Bollinger moving average. A speculator can enter the market when the previous extreme has been overtaken (point 6), because the pattern has been reclassified as parallels on the basis of several criteria. In a situation like this, it is imperative to use support/resistance levels of the control unit of time as a stop-loss during the T2, T3 and T4 periods of the major unit of time.

Dynamic Analysis of Parallels

In most cases, the presence of parallels on a given unit of time leads to the formation of a bubble on the next unit of time up. However, parallels can be propagated to several units of time, especially in sub-hourly units. As a general rule, you should reckon that upstream and downstream of a bubble/parallels pattern, you might find another type of configuration.

Table 5.1 summarizes the effect on the principal and control units of time of the Bollinger moving average observed on the major unit of time.

In the right-hand part of Figure 5.7, when T2 appears on the daily chart, the market is at T0 on the next unit of time up. T2 appears on the weekly chart, at point 1, as soon as the top of T1 is crossed upwards. The trader will take a buy position. Prices are at 2 on the next unit of time down. On the daily chart, prices shadow the upper band and parallels are to be expected. The most probable pattern to

Table 5.1   Dynamic approach for parallels and bubble.

	Flat Bollinger moving average*	Weakly trending moving average	Strong moving average	
Control unit of time	stable	unusable parallels	parallels or other	parallels
Major unit of time	flat curves	no figure	parallels	bubble
Main unit of time	flat curves weak trend	other	bubble	other

* On the major unit of time.

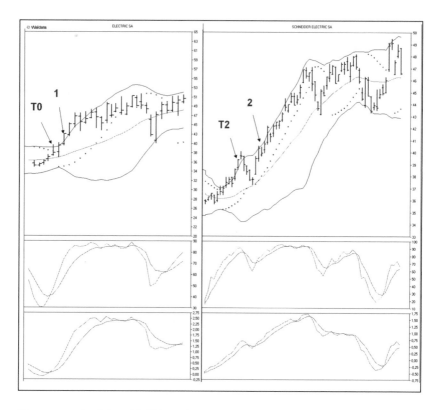

Figure 5.7   Parallels and bubble on the next unit of time up.

emerge on the weekly chart is a bubble, and the continuation of the chart will confirm this later.

5.3. Pre-parallels

Features

This figure forms when prices move from one Bollinger band to the other and then move back as far as the Bollinger moving average without crossing it. In the initial phase, the Bollinger moving average presents a trend opposite to those of the stochastic and the MACD. In the following phase the Bollinger moving average stabilizes. Prices use the Bollinger moving average as a support/resistance level. If the trend continues as far as the parabolic, the following movement will be smaller in scope.

Note that the presence of this pattern does not mean you can look for a bigger than expected swing with conventional parallels, because it is encountered when the Bollinger bands are wide apart.

Management

With this configuration you can take up a position amounting to 70% of the position allowed for parallels. The remainder is purchased once the parallels have been confirmed. The end of a non-crossover on the MACD tells speculators thay can take out a position.

In Figure 5.8, the MACD is oversold at point A but the Bollinger moving average at point 1 is trending down and you are not advised to go long here. At point 2, the Bollinger moving average has stabilized and prices, which have not crossed the upper Bollinger band, are moving down in the direction of the moving average. At point 3, the double parabolic and Bollinger moving average support has not been crossed by prices. Moreover, the Bollinger moving average is trending upwards. As soon as the non-crossover on the MACD is finished at point B, the speculator adopts a buy position at point 4 as bullish parallels are expected.

5.4. Non-parallels

For parallels to arise, there must be no upsets. Aberrations are mostly noticed on intraday or daily charts.

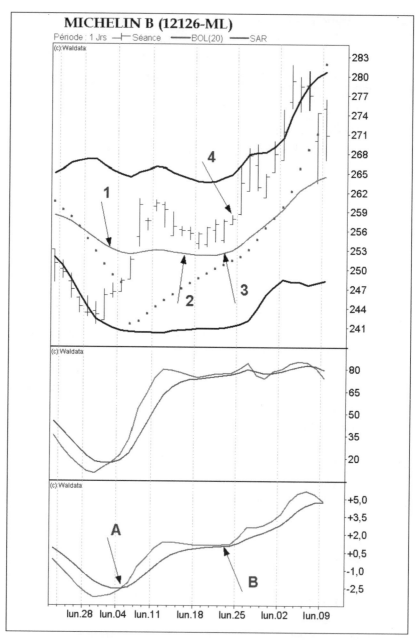

Figure 5.8 Pre-parallels.

Quotes for a currency pair like such as euro/NOK have no significant impact in the Far East. Similarly, when the markets open, foreign news items may be taken into account and generate short-lived reactions. An analysis from the point of view of the acceleration of the movement and its impact on various units of time makes it possible to "measure" the scale of the phenomenon.

Of course, the acceleration factors listed as part of the conditions needed to trigger parallels also apply fully to this section.

Mechanical factors should also be taken into account.

Bollinger band divergence is clearly an essential condition if we wish to talk of parallels. Similarly, we must make certain that there are no support/resistance levels on neighbouring units of time. If this concerns the next unit of time down, it is less important than on the next unit up. On the other hand, the probability of seeing parallels form increases if the support/resistance level on the next unit of time up is exceeded, which happens frequently.

At point T4 in the left-hand part of Figure 5.9, the Bollinger bands are undeniably symmetrical. The market still has considerable acceleration potential. On the other hand, at point T4 on the right, the Bollinger bands are not symmetrical. The uptrend is almost over.

5.5. Impact of a Divergence on the Bollinger Bands

A divergence of the stochastic and the MACD corresponds to a trend reversal. The minimum target is thus the Bollinger moving average if the divergence only concerns the stochastic. If divergence is also observed on the MACD, the opposite Bollinger band becomes the minimum target. Finally, if the divergence only concerns the MACD, the target must be sought on the next unit of time up. The most probable chart pattern is the formation of parallels. Sometimes a divergence is followed by a halt on the Bollinger moving average, signifying that a very strong new trend is about

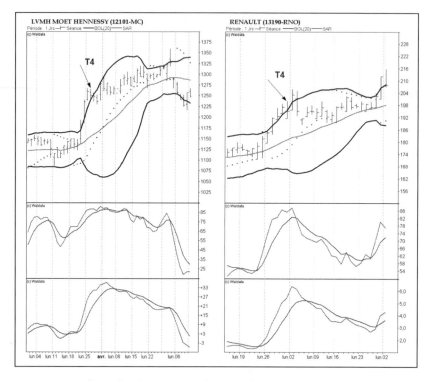

Figure 5.9   Bollinger band symmetry at the time of a divergence.

to begin in the opposite direction. This generally signals the emergence of pre-parallels.

5.6. Non-divergence of Bollinger Bands

One essential condition for parallels is that the two Bollinger bands have to diverge. If the bands do not diverge, this means that there is no increased price volatility and therefore that the probability of seeing an increase in price fluctuations is virtually nil. One particular thing that is noted when the Bollinger bands are flat is that prices move for a period outside the Bollinger bands. Yet the opposite band remains flat. In such cases, even if T1 forms, it is rare to see the move continue into the subsequent period. On the contrary, we generally note a closure inside the Bollinger band. At the same time, or during the subsequent periods, the stochastic becomes overbought/oversold and the price reverses.

5.7. Semi-bubble

General Features

A semi-bubble starts exactly like an ordinary bubble. But as of T2, one of the two bands stagnates or continues to diverge very slowly.

Dynamic Aspect

A semi-bubble is preceded on the control unit of time by unusable parallel bands.

Tracking your Position

So long as the stochastic is not overbought when the main trend is bullish or oversold when the main trend is bearish, investors and speculators will hold their positions.

During T1 and T2 in Figure 5.10, the upper Bollinger band has moved sharply, whereas the lower Bollinger band has moved only slowly. Sometimes there is no crossover between the parabolic and the Bollinger moving average. To unwind the position, you simply need to wait until the stochastic is overbought at point A.

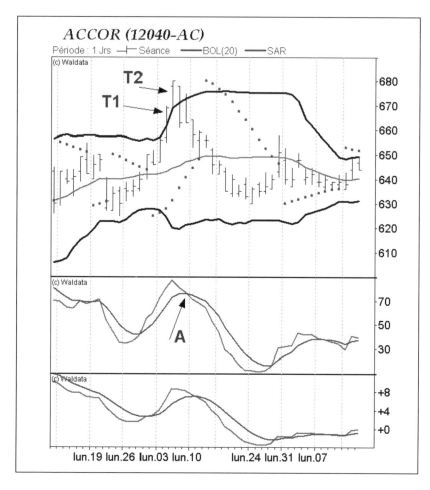

Figure 5.10   Semi-bubble.

5.8. Non-semi-bubble

If one of the two Bollinger bands remains flat and does not mark the start of a trend, we cannot really talk of a semi-bubble. In Figure 5.11, the upper Bollinger band is still flatlining when the acceleration takes place during 1. There is thus no semi-bubble and even less formation of parallels.

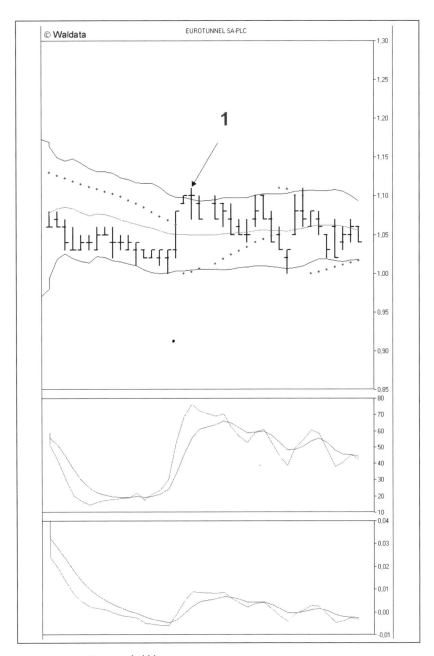

Figure 5.11 Non-semi-bubble.

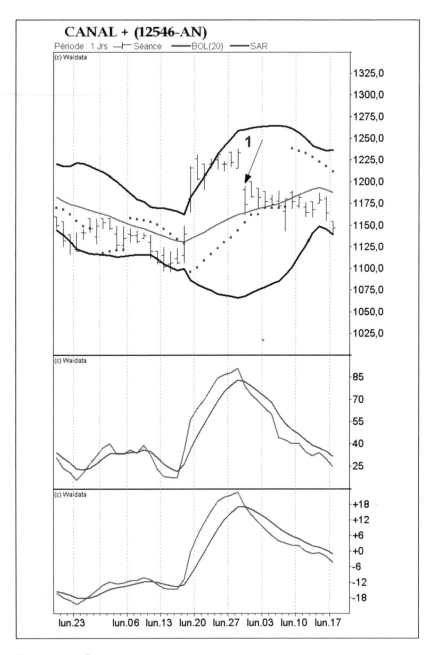

Figure 5.12 Gaps.

5.9. Graphical Pattern: Gap

A gap is a price differential observed on two opposing extremes between one period and the next. A gap can be bullish or bearish and has two possible causes: a lack of liquidity in the market which triggers a price trend; or an imbalance between supply and demand. The latter case is more frequently encountered. It occurs in intraday trading, following the publication of a news item (generally of an economic nature) or the start of a new business day in response to trading on other markets. These gaps can be powerful and sometimes undermine the previous trend, even if the current chart shows a pattern of parallels.

In Figure 5.12, the gap that appears at point 1 signals a trend reversal. The position must be unwound as the end of the period is approaching, because when a market opens with a gap, if the gap is not closed during that period, a new trend is in the offing. If the gap is closed during the period, it means that the movement observed at the start of trading was only technical. Subsequently, the earlier trend should come back into its own.

Chapter **6**

How to Take a Position

Managers will use a monthly, weekly or daily triptych for their analyses. Speculators will find opportunities on all units of time from monthly to five minutes. Speculation must not therefore be confused with short-term trades.

6.1. Managers = Use of Stochastic and MACD

Once the investor has decided which major unit of time he prefers, he only has to keep an eye on the stochastic and the MACD to take a position. This is done in two stages:

- On the major unit of time, at the start of the period, wait until you see a crossover between the MACD and its moving average which confirms the one observed between the stochastic and its moving average.
- On the control unit of time, watch out for the figure formed by the stochastic and its moving average. If %K and %D are parallel (moving in the direction of the stochastic and the major unit of time) and if the MACD has just crossed its moving average, this is the ideal situation, and the manager will take out a position (see Figure 6.1). If it is likely that over the following three periods, %K

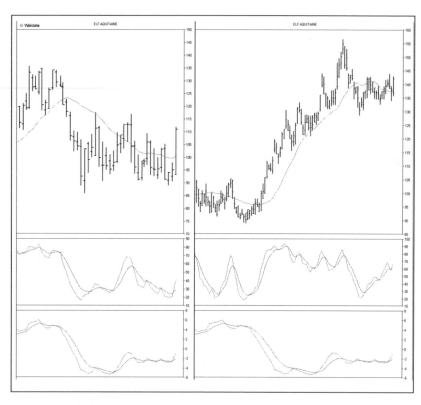

Figure 6.1 Ideal situation.

will not cross %D, this is also an acceptable pattern for taking out a position (see Figure 6.2).

On the other hand, if a trend reversal is likely in one of the two coming periods, traders should avoid taking a position (see Figure 6.3). They should wait until the stochastic and then the MACD are once more overbought/oversold on the control unit of time. In this case, the trader should make sure that the signals are still valid on the major unit of time.

On the left in Figure 6.4, the major unit of time is weekly. At point A the stochastic is oversold. At point B, one week later, the MACD is also oversold. As soon as the MACD is oversold on the

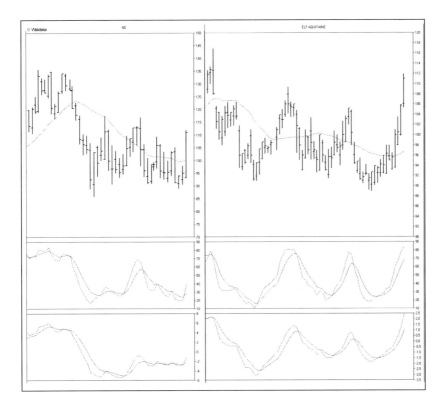

Figure 6.2   Acceptable case.

control unit of time (daily, right), an investor should take a position if the stochastic shows that the ongoing move retains a degree of potential.

When crossover B takes place, on the daily unit of time, the market is at point 1, and the stochastic at C′. The stochastic and MACD have just become oversold. In practice, this is the ideal condition for taking a position. If the stochastic had been at point I, the trader would have had to wait for the next oversold state of the MACD at point D. The moving average is trending upward. The straight line drawn on the price (2–3) is diverging with that on the stochastic (F–G). A price drop is expected. At point D the MACD is oversold. You need to compare the crossover at point D with the previous oversold state, C.

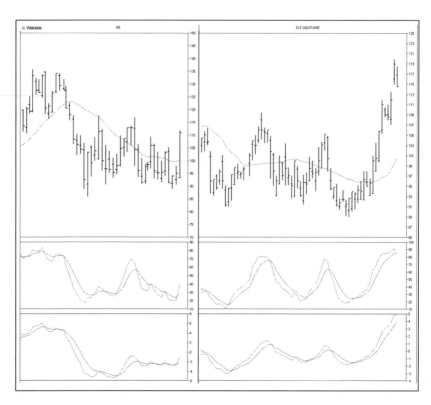

Figure 6.3   To be avoided.

The straight line linking the two lows is moving up and a straight line drawn between points 0 and 4 is also rising. The correction that occurred between points 3 and 4 has ended. The price starts to rise again from point D. You can now buy or increase your position because the weekly MACD is still running parallel to its moving average at point J. Similarly, at point E on the daily MACD, a non-crossover is visible. As the MACD on the major unit of time has just become oversold, the risk taken by a trader who buys into the market is low. This case also constitutes a buy opportunity if no position has been taken at point B.

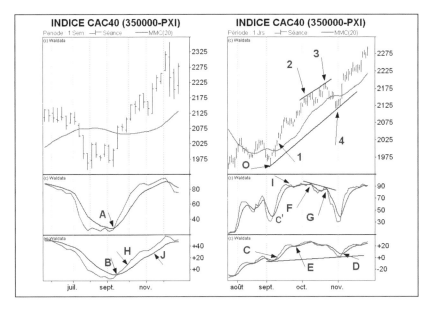

Figure 6.4   Major unit of time and control unit of time.

6.2. Speculators/Opportunity Seeking = Waiting for T2

A speculator takes a position when parallels are expected on the major unit of time or if they are effective on the control unit of time. The aim of speculative trades is to look for opportunities and take advantage of large-scale price shifts to generate capital gains.

In Figure 6.5, between points 1 and 2 the Bollinger bands are flat and close together for nine periods. During T1, a gap is visible and we have an acceleration between the opening and closing prices as well as a symmetrical divergence on the Bollinger bands. During the following period (T2), as soon as the previous high of T1 is overtaken by three ticks, a buy position is taken.

Price differentials can occur during very short periods of a few minutes. In this case, the trader can take his profit in less than 30 minutes. But the period can also last several months or even several

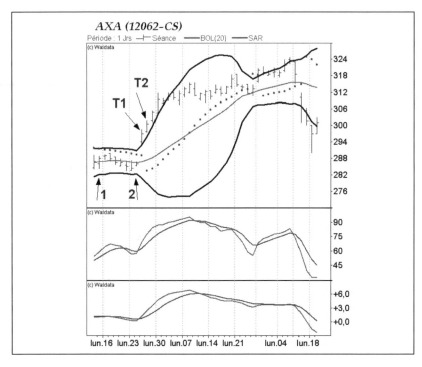

Figure 6.5   Parallels/bubble.

years, as shown by several ongoing examples on various markets. It all depends on the units of time chosen when trading. However, the main strength of DTAFM® is the fact that, while you can use principal, major and control units of time as short as ten, five, or even one minute, the method can be just as easily applied with monthly, weekly or daily units of time without any kind of distortion. No other approach allows you to use a single method for such an extended forecasting time frame with such high levels of reliability.

Trading in Real Time and Deferred Time

We can draw a distinction between two kinds of trader: those with real-time software, and those who only obtain daily updates. The cost of a real-time data feed can only be justified for portfolios of over USD 200 000, and for traders who can spend several hours a day in front of their screens. This means that for lesser-value portfolios, trading should only take place using trading lead times of between one and three weeks (i.e. a weekly major unit of time). Conversely, traders using real-time software can use a period of ten minutes as their major unit of time. This means they can unwind a position on a currency or futures contract between 30 minutes and two hours after buying into the market thanks to the possibility of having orders executed in less than one minute. The same reasoning applies, of course, to foreign exchange and futures trading. The use of a five-minute major unit of time and a one-minute control unit of time makes this method an outstanding aid for professional speculators.

The emergence of deferred real time means a new category of speculator can enter the field: individual speculators. These are people who want to generate capital gains over periods of a few days, while only checking out their software once a day (this is the basic need of most individuals who use technical analysis). They will use a weekly, daily and hourly triptych. They will have opportunities of finding many signals related to the speculation/stock-picking option without increasing the cost of using their software and staying glued to their screens. There are more possibilities using a daily, hourly and half-hourly triptych, but this demands greater availability because of the need to analyse the triptych twice a day. Moreover, the availability of the 30-minute chart with a time lag of half an hour can make using the method a chore.

Taking a Position

All the criteria listed when I defined dynamic analysis and parallels should be looked for so as to detect parallel patterns as quickly as possible when analysing a triptych.

Management

Two cases should be taken into account depending on whether the parallels are in the control unit of time or the major unit of time.

Control unit of time

This is the most favourable case a trader can encounter. A bubble, reflected in an acceleration, is expected on the major unit of time. If the Bollinger bands are still flat on the major unit of time, you should invest up to your authorized ceiling during T2 on the major unit of time. If a position has already been taken on the major unit of time, it will need to be increased as soon as possible (investors).

Major unit of time

If parallels (T2) become visible on the major unit of time, the criterion is weighted 100 and the coefficient is 80. All types of traders know how to take a position on the basis of specific criteria. Positions are managed in the same way by all traders.

Chapter 7

Tracking a Position and Unwinding It

Investors who have taken a position can be confronted with three different situations: a stable market; weak price fluctuations; and a large-scale trend (the trend of the Bollinger moving average and the price situation compared to the Bollinger bands are used as selection criteria). In the case of a large-scale price trend, investors put on their speculators' hats as soon as T2 is visible so as to optimize the unwinding of their positions.

Speculators are generally only concerned with the third situation. In practice, however, they can be confronted with the first two cases, because once they have taken a position, a market does not always develop with the expected strength. They must therefore know how to deal with a situation that was not expected at the outset, to cut out of a position and where necessary take the hit when the criteria expected for the following trend are absent or contradicted.

The problem is always the same for investors and speculators alike: what do I need to do to turn a profit?

7.1. Stable Market: Stochastic

Flat Bollinger Moving Average

The stochastic is the most useful aid for monitoring the market. A trend continues as long as the stochastic is not overbought/oversold. Semi-bubbles also belong in this category.

In practice, when investors see flat Bollinger bands on the principal unit of time, they may possibly develop a strategy aimed at selling volatility. As long as prices stay inside the Bollinger bands on the major unit of time, they will maintain their position. If T2 begins, they will change strategy.

If the stochastic on the major unit of time shows a divergence, a trend reversal is possible if the opposite Bollinger band is not used as a support/resistance level. At that point it is advisable to unwind any open positions or get ready to take up a position according to the type of divergence and on the basis of the management rules.

At point A in Figure 7.1, an investor can sell volatility since the moving average and the Bollinger bands are flat. An investor/speculator with a long position could sell it in A at the crossover between the stochastic and its moving average. At point 2 care is required, because this period could be identified as T1. However, during the subsequent period, the low is not breached and there are no concerns about parallels forming. A price pick-up towards the upper Bollinger band is consequently expected. An investor/speculator with a short position could buy it back at B at the crossover between the stochastic and its moving average.

End of a Semi-bubble

In the case of a semi-bubble, the position must be unwound as soon as the stochastic becomes overbought or oversold. The Bollinger bands or the parabolic will often be used as targets on the next unit of time up.

7.2. Weak or Medium Trend: MACD

Prices stay inside the Bollinger bands and you should not observe a T2 period. In times of rise or fall, the MACD is the model that will

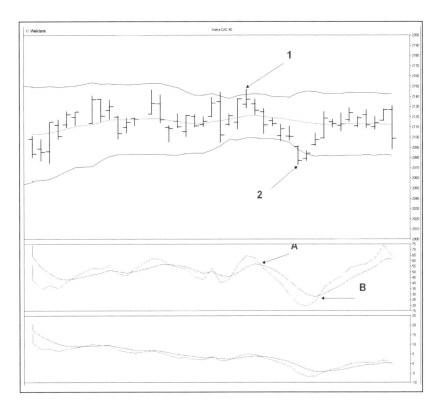

Figure 7.1 Using the stochastic.

allow you to forecast market behaviour most effectively. The trend will continue for as long as the MACD is not overbought/oversold.

If the MACD on the major unit of time reveals a divergence, a change of trend is accordingly expected. You should unwind your position and take up a buy or sell position depending on the type of divergence and according to the management rules.

If the MACD is overbought/oversold, the management rules must be applied on the basis of the major unit of time involved.

With the pattern seen in Figure 7.2, an investor took up a buy position at point A when the crossover of the stochastic on the major unit of time was confirmed by the MACD at point A. On the hourly control unit of time, not shown here, an MACD crossover occurred

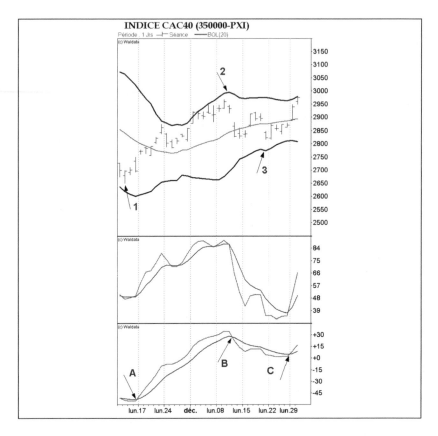

Figure 7.2 Using the MACD.

simultaneously. As the Bollinger moving average on the major unit of time was bullish, the investor waited until the MACD was over-bought at point B before unwinding the position taken at point A.

7.3. Strong or Very Strong Trend: Bollinger Bands

Prices break out of the Bollinger bands. As soon as the T2 state is visible, the investor must act like a speculator who is going to have to manage a bubble or parallels. The pattern of parallels that are non-usable by speculators will be dealt with as if they were classic parallels.

If prices continue to shadow the Bollinger band closely, or if the parabolic crosses the Bollinger moving average when the Bollinger bands diverge, there is a high probability of seeing parallels. Conversely, if prices move outside, a bubble can be forecast.

Where a bubble exists, you must always remember that it could be reclassified as parallels.

Parallels

The parabolic and the Bollinger moving average will be used to close out the position. Fifty per cent of the position is sold when the first indicator is overtaken, and the remaining 50% unwound when the other indicator is overtaken in its turn.

Generally speaking, the parabolic is crossed before the moving average. As soon as the parabolic is crossed, 50% of the position is sold. For the remaining 50%, the question is whether to take your profits during the same period when the moving average is crossed, or only when the closing price is on the opposite side of the Bollinger moving average. Experience tells us to break the order into two equal parts. The first order is given as soon as the moving average is crossed, while the second is executed when the closing price is on the opposite side of the moving average.

Confronted with Figure 7.3, an investor took a buy position at 1216 once the oversold status of the weekly MACD was confirmed by upwardly biased parallels on the daily chart (not shown here). A speculator took a long position during the period T2 (point 1). The bullish movement on the weekly chart transforms into parallels when the parabolic crosses the Bollinger moving average at a time when the Bollinger bands are still moving apart. No plateau phase can be

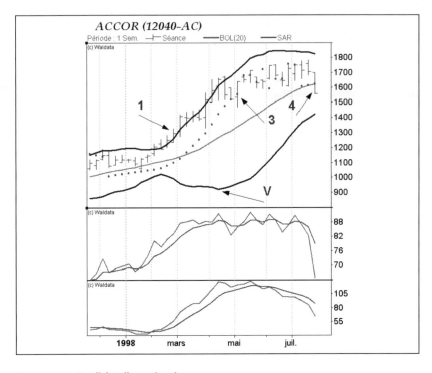

Figure 7.3   Parallel Bollinger bands.

observed on the opposite band when it reverses at point V. Fifty per cent of the position was sold at point 3 when the price crossed the parabolic. The rest of the position was held until point 4 when the price crossed the Bollinger moving average. In the present case, managing the position on the basis of unwinding rules for parallel patterns offers no great improvement in comparison with the results obtained using conventional management methods. However, as we saw before, you can achieve substantially better results by selling 50% of the position when the price crosses the parabolic and selling another 25% when the price crosses the Bollinger moving average. The remaining 25% will be sold when the market closes below the Bollinger moving average.

Bubble

Exiting from a bubble

The market is about to fluctuate rapidly. As a general rule, if the trend is too strong at the outset, the acceleration is unlikely to continue. On the other hand, the steadier the move, the longer the bubble should continue. As long as the plateau phase continues, prices are likely to continue trending provided the stochastic is not overbought (bullish market) or oversold (bearish market). The current trend on the major unit of time (daily or weekly) will continue until the Bollinger moving average of the control unit of time is crossed. If the major unit of time is hourly or sub-hourly, the control unit of time's moving average will be replaced by the opposite Bollinger band.

When a trader is not sure whether the opposite band has reversed, he should watch the stochastic. An overbought/oversold state here confirms the trend reversal. Generally speaking, the stochastic becomes overbought/oversold just after the reversal of the opposite Bollinger band. The crossover of the parabolic and the Bollinger moving average also indicates the presence of a top/bottom in a recent period.

In Figure 7.4, when the opposite band reverses at point 1, the price is at point 2. The capital gain in relation to T2 is considerable. Sometimes, the break-out at point 1 is not so pronounced because the curve is rounded. The crossover at point A on the stochastic confirms that the opposite band has effectively changed direction. Note a price high when the parabolic crosses the moving average.

Continuation of price trend

Subsequently, several possible situations may emerge:

Neither the parabolic nor the Bollinger moving average is crossed[1]

Limited technical correction/recovery.　In this case, the price changes direction once more before it reaches the parabolic. You take out a

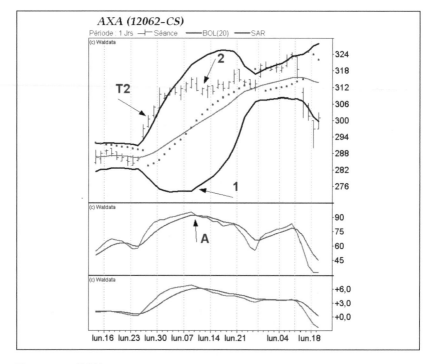

Figure 7.4 Bubble.

new position during the period where the new trend reversal has been observed if there is a strong probability of a closing price outside the opposite of the top/bottom in the preceding period. You manage the new position according to the rules of parallels.

In Figure 7.5, a correction begins at point 1 and continues until point 2. The parabolic has not been crossed. During the period following point 2, as soon as there is a probability that the closing price will break out beyond the top in the previous period, you buy. Fifty per cent of the position is sold when the price crosses the parabolic (point 3), and the remaining 50% is sold, in two equal trades, when the price crosses the Bollinger moving average (points 4 and 5).

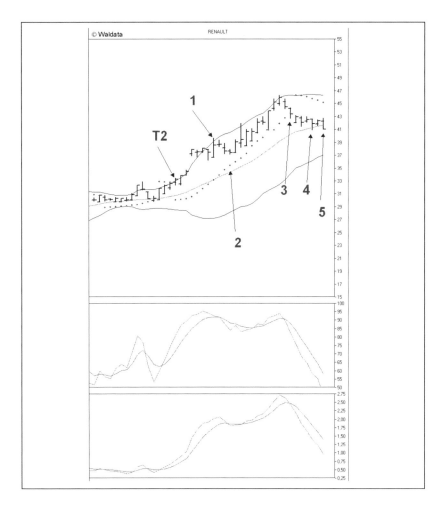

Figure 7.5   Limited technical correction.

The same trend continues after crossover between the parabolic and the Bollinger moving average.   If the trend observed before the crossover between the parabolic and the Bollinger moving average continues during the period following the one after the crossover, traders who do not have open positions can take advantage of this opportunity to buy into the market. The situation is managed as if we had a pattern of parallels.

In Figure 7.6, during the period following the one after the cross-over between the parabolic and the Bollinger moving average, at point 1, the bullish trend continues. During the subsequent period, a buy position is taken because there is a strong probability of seeing a closing top higher than the previous one. The position will be managed in the same way as for parallels. Fifty per cent of the position is sold when the price crosses the parabolic (point 2), and the remaining 50% is sold, in two equal trades, when the price crosses the Bollinger moving average.

Either the parabolic or the Bollinger moving average is crossed

During the correction (following a bullish trend reversal on the opposite band) or the recovery (in the opposing case), if one only

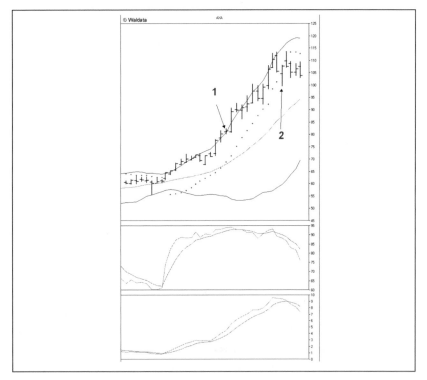

Figure 7.6   Reserve of power.

of the indicators has been crossed, the market will move back towards the earlier top. This level is often difficult to break out of. If this level does not act as a resistance level, the trend will continue towards the closer Bollinger band if the stochastic has not become overbought (the opposite band is rising) or oversold (the opposite band is falling). When the price touches the Bollinger band, a trend reversal is expected and the rest of the position should be unwound.

In Figure 7.7 prices are shadowing the lower Bollinger band and the pattern is assimilated to parallels. When the price crosses the parabolic at point 1, 50% of the position is purchased. The remaining 50% is bought at point 2 when the level of the previous bottom

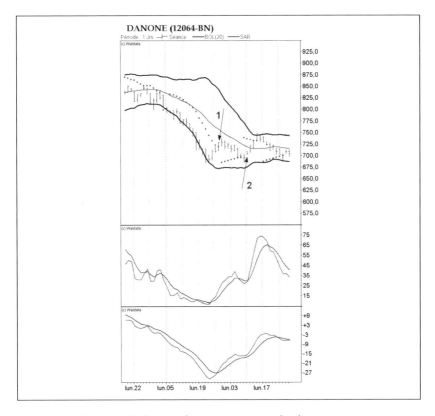

Figure 7.7   The parabolic does not function as a support level.

resists. The present case is fairly rare. In general, the parabolic serves as a support/resistance level.

The two indicators are crossed

When the plateau phase on the opposite band is finished (the stochastic crosses its moving average and the parabolic crosses the Bollinger moving average), the price trend reverses. Prices will start moving towards the opposite Bollinger band as soon as the parabolic and the moving average have been crossed. This move is rapid and I would advise against taking a position if the chart is not a weekly or monthly one.

Detecting the end of parallels and bubbles is simple since the criteria are fully determined. Before transmitting an order, it is important to get organized. The following chapter introduces a document designed to help you do just that.

Note

1. The information given here is difficult to exploit. Beginners should avoid trying to use it.

Chapter 8

Implementation

It is mainly when the market suddenly starts trending strongly that mistakes can be expensive. For a speculator, it is better to miss out on a trend some of whose characteristics are different from those described here, than to take a position that corresponds neither to parallels nor a bubble.

When an overbought or oversold state is visible on a weekly major unit of time, investors can take a position, with a degree of risk, if they have recently observed a type 1 or 2 crossover in the same direction on the daily stochastic. This is because in this case it is not certain that, at the time of the next overbought/oversold state on the major unit of time, the move will have the same amplitude as the previous one. This comment does not hold true for shorter units of time. The rule regarding confirmation of an overbought/oversold state on the control unit of time must be scrupulously observed. To familiarize yourself with the various cases, there is nothing like practising with historic series.

I suggest you print out a large number of old triptychs and put them to one side so that you can analyse them at leisure. Subsequently, you can check whether you were right by using your software to check how the markets have moved.

Before taking a position, you have to draw up a plan so that you can compare the various stocks, indices, etc., and, among the stocks you pick, set buy and sell levels.

The master plan is a document that will help you draw up a *modus operandi* summarizing your objectives and the action to take.

8.1. Master Plan

I have already explained why the analysis has to be carried out using the triptych. The parabolic and the Bollinger bands serve as support and resistance levels.

An example of a master plan is presented in Table 8.1. P is the parabolic, U the upper Bollinger band, M the Bollinger moving average and L the lower band. For the different units of time, M stands for monthly, W weekly, D daily and H hourly; for sub-hourly units of time, use the corresponding number of minutes.

These symbols can be combined so that MW stands for the Bollinger moving average on a chart with a weekly unit of time, MM stands for the Bollinger moving average on a chart with a monthly unit of time, L5 stands for the lower Bollinger band on a chart with a five-minute unit of time and UD stands for the upper Bollinger band on a chart with a daily unit of time.

The objectives are given in the XY columns. The numerical values are given for information purposes only, as these were the values when the analysis was carried out. I have given a maximum of three levels for support and resistance levels. Any comments should be no more than ten words long and indicate the action to take. Forecasts in this master plan are monthly.

Support and Resistance Levels

Support and resistance levels are selected moving gradually away from the latest available price. You will make your selection not only on the major unit of time but also on the principal unit of time and

Table 8.1 Monthly forecast.*

Instrument	Support	XY	Resistance	XY	January 1998 comments
CAC 40	2886 2780	MW LD	3274 3104	UM PM	BULLISH IF > PM = RISE IN 1998 BEARISH IF < MW
DOW JONES US	7413 6944	LW LM	8662 8266	UM PM	BULLISH IF > PM = RISE FOR 1998
SP 500	932 881	LD PM	1040 990	UM UD	BULLISH IF > UD
DAX	4039 3967	MW LD	4688 4428	UM PM	BULLISH IF > PM = RISE FOR 1998
FT 100	5027	MW	5414 5353	UM PM	BULLISH IF > PM = RISE FOR 1998
NIKKEI	14 316 14 295 —	LW LOW	16 703 15 845	MW MD	SHARP FALL IN 1998
HANG SENG	9864 8391 —	LD LW	12 186	MD	CORRECTION IF < LD FALL IF < LW
AS UD GOLD PM FIXING	279 —	LW	297	UD	SHARP FALL SO LONG = RESISTANCE
DOWNWARD BUBBLE LIGHT CRUDE WTI MARCH	17.28 —	LM	18.53	MD	MONTHLY IF < LM

Ph. CAHEN telephone +33 1 49 24 77 02. E-mail: cahen@dcmc.creditlyonnais.fr

*This table was available during January 1998 on the Crédit Lyonnais website (www.finance.creditlyonnais.fr) on the Economic and Financial Research Division/ Technical Analysis page.

the control unit of time. The objectives located on the control unit of time are less significant than those on the principal unit of time.

If the market is trending very strongly, you can indicate this by suggesting only a resistance or a support level. If two indicators on the same unit of time are located at an identical level, you should focus on the Bollinger bands. If you observe the same level on two different units of time, you should select the one located on the longer unit of time. When drawing up the plan, you should start by filling in your XY objectives, then the comments, and then finally the numerical values. This ensures that you are not influenced by values that are being circulated or which may have a psychological influence on the analyst.

Comments

Comments will be based on observation of unusual factors. Once the triptych has been studied, an analyst will either use the comments as a reference for his own action if he is trading on his own behalf, or will pass on the study to the traders. Whatever the case, the comments should help participants take speedy decisions. Nothing should be done in a trendless market. In this case, simply note "trendless market". If the Bollinger moving average is trending up or down on the major unit of time, but if the Bollinger bands show neither parallels nor a bubble, your comment should be "bullish so long as MY is being used as a support or bearish so long as it serves as a resistance level", Y being the unit of time on which the observation was carried out. Generally speaking, comments refer to the major unit of time. However, if a divergence, a bubble or parallels form on another unit of time, it is a good idea to point this out and to say what the main target will be: in general, one of the Bollinger bands on the next unit of time up. Similarly, you need to indicate the level when the existence of a trend is called into doubt. For example, a crossover on the moving average at the end of the month should be flagged. Indicate the numerical level that confirms the presence of parallels (T2).

My method differs from most others in that it uses an objective approach. This means that when confronted with a triptych, all users of this version of DTAFM$^{®}$ will formulate the same hypotheses. The most important thing to my mind is that you have learned to work with a method and can apply it consistently. You will have learned to trust the models and your own judgement, for a very reasonable intellectual investment.

If you miss the beginning of a trend, wait for the upstream signals that will enable you to take the contrary position if a trend reversal is forecast. Sometimes, the move can spread to higher units of time, so that you can take up a position when the required trading criteria are present once more. Whatever the case, for good performance, it is better to do nothing when the signals are unclear or contradictory.

The patterns presented in the next few pages are met with regularly. Before trading, you have to be able to detect them when you meet them.

8.2. Analysing a Triptych

When it comes to analysing a triptych, the approach is the same for investors and speculators alike. You need to construct the future history of the particular market. To do so, you must be able, once you have detected the unusual component, to work out what this might mean, basing your view on the major unit of time and the principal unit of time. When several unusual components are present, you will need to prioritize them according to the unit of time in which you observed them and decide whether their impact is cumulative or whether they partly offset each other.

The objective is to make a three-week forecast from Figure 8.1. On the principal unit of time, the Bollinger moving average is bullish, whereas the stochastic is oversold and a non-crossover has occurred on the MACD. On the major unit of time, the stochastic and the MACD are both oversold and an acceleration has enabled the price to break out of the upper Bollinger band. In the control unit of time, unusable parallels have formed. The trend is bullish. On the weekly chart, parallels will form if the price closes above the upper Bollinger band and if the following week this week's high is overtopped.

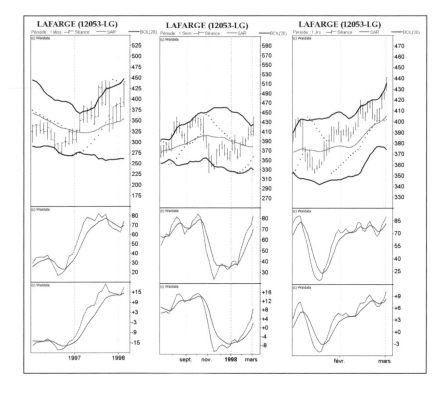

Figure 8.1   Triptych for analysis.

The divergence of the Bollinger bands, the rise in the parabolic and the start of a non-crossover two weeks previously on the weekly stochastic mean you can forecast the formation of these parallels. If this pattern does form, the bullish trend visible on the stochastic and the monthly MACD will be strengthened. On the basis of this assumption, the rise will continue on the weekly chart so long as the plateau phase continues. A price rise of several weeks' duration is thus expected. Moreover, if the weekly lower Bollinger band reverses to a bullish stance without an initial plateau phase, speculators will hold their buy positions while the parabolic or the Bollinger moving average acts as a support level. Once the bullish trend has been validated (the following week), it will only be called into doubt if the daily Bollinger moving average does not act as a support level over the next three weeks. Given the fact that prices are accelerating upwards, this hypothesis is relatively unlikely.

In Figure 8.2, on the weekly major unit of time at point T2, an acceleration has actually taken place. A few weeks later, the opposite Bollinger band has reversed upwards, whereas the plateau phase at point 1 was of short duration. Furthermore, after period T2, prices have shadowed the upper Bollinger band. There is consequently a strong probability that parallels have formed. This probability is further strengthened by the fact that the parabolic and the moving average have been crossed, whereas the Bollinger bands are diverging. On 13 July 1998, 50% of the position was sold at point 2 and

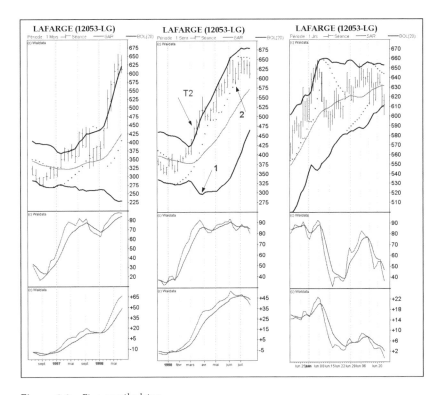

Figure 8.2 Five months later.

the remaining 50% will be sold when the price crosses the Bollinger moving average. However, the proximity of LD will prompt you to close out the position at this level if this support does not hold.

8.3. Conclusion

You should now know how to use the tools that will allow you to forecast future trends. Using a triptych, you can work out how prices are likely to move over the coming periods. The DTAFM® method means there is no need to be hampered by limited objectives, as you can imagine other scenarios. You can therefore combine safety with the possibility of following the markets into unexplored territory.

If you have any enquiry for the author, please send an e-mail to atdmfpc@voila.fr

Index